By including ecological concerns in the design process from the outset, architecture can enhance life. Author Brook Muller understands how a designer's predispositions and poetic judgement in dealing with complex and dynamic ecological systems impact the "greenness" of built outcomes. *Ecology and the Architectural Imagination* offers a series of speculations on architectural possibility when ecology is embedded from conceptual phases onward, how notions of function and structure of ecosystems can inspire ideas of architectural space making and order, and how the architect's role and contribution can shift through this engagement. As an ecological architect working in increasingly dense urban environments, you can create diverse spaces of inhabitation and connect project-scale living systems with those at the neighborhood and region scales. Equipped with ecological literacy, critical thinking and collaboration skills, you are empowered to play important roles in the remaking of our cities.

Brook Muller is Associate Dean of the School of Architecture and Allied Arts, Associate Professor of Architecture, Director of the Graduate Certificate Program in Ecological Design and core faculty member of the Environmental Studies Program at the University of Oregon, USA.

Ecology

and the

Architectural Imagination

Brook Muller

Routledge
Taylor & Francis Group

NEW YORK AND LONDON

First published 2014
by Routledge
711 Third Avenue, New York, NY 10017

and by Routledge
2 Park Square, Milton Park, Abingdon, Oxon OX14 4RN

Routledge is an imprint of the Taylor & Francis Group, an informa business

Library of Congress Cataloging in Publication Data
Muller, Brook.
  Ecology and the architectural imagination / Brook Muller.
  pages cm
  Includes bibliographical references and index.
  1. Architectural design. 2. Architecture–Environmental aspects.
  3. Sustainable archtecture. I. Title.
  A2750.M85 2014
  720'.47–dc23

                                                 2013032288

ISBN: 978-0-415-62274-5 (hbk)
ISBN: 978-0-415-62275-2 (pbk)
ISBN: 978-1-315-81692-0 (ebk)

Acquisition Editor: Wendy Fuller
Editorial Assistant: Emma Gadsden
Production Editor: Ed Gibbons

Typeset in Frutiger and Galliard
by Wearset Ltd, Boldon, Tyne and Wear

MIX
Paper from
responsible sources
FSC
www.fsc.org   FSC® C013056

Printed and bound in Great Britain by
TJ International Ltd, Padstow, Cornwall

Humanity's entry into the Era of Cities necessitates an ecologically regenerative urbanism. Brook Muller is one of its greatest pioneers.

Robert F. Young, *Assistant Professor at University of Texas*

This is the luminous re-imagining of architectural possibility that the reeling world deeply needs, a turn from an anthropocentric to an ecocentric ethos.

Kathleen Dean Moore, *co-editor,*
Moral Ground: Ethical Action for a Planet in Peril

A stimulating impulse directing architecture beyond green design to a far broader conversation with natural, political, metaphorical, and historical ecologies.

W. S. K. Cameron, *PhD, Loyola Marymount University*

Recognizing that the very meaning of ecological and sustainable design is an open-ended imaginative experiment, Muller perceptively examines a number of metaphors for framing design concepts conducive to helping humans, non-humans, and ecosystems flourish together.

Mark Johnson, *Philip H. Knight Professor of Liberal Arts and Sciences, University of Oregon and author of* The Meaning of the Body, *and* Metaphors We Live By

Contents

Part III

Ecoarchitectural Strategies and Orders 103

Preface

By focusing design expression on natural systems processes augmented by the human hand, through timely engagement of ecological methods, models and metaphors, architects through their collaborative efforts can expand ideas of the performance of the city. A deeply ecological architectural intervention is one that creates more diverse urban habitat frameworks, filters and cleanses stormwater in order to improve biological conditions in compromised waterways, fortifies the connective ecological tissue of neighborhoods and regions, and in other ways supports broader, regenerative landscape processes. To engage these possibilities is to excite the architectural imaginary, accept higher levels of unpredictability, and invite heightened aesthetic speculation.

Each chapter offers a vignette of the life of architecture in the realm of ecology; these can be read in sequence or independently. Subjects shift between conceptions of environmental problems and problems of design conception. Part I (Chapters 1–3), "Ecological architectures within a broader context," looks to the value of comprehensive environmental problem formulation as a set up for architectural thinking, the challenges of aligning design and ecological agendas in stitching projects into the fabric of the city, and the architectural implications of different models of ecosystem behavior. Part II (Chapters 4–7), "Conceptual (eco)architectural constructs," addresses the role of metaphor in architectural design and explores implications of appropriating and reinterpreting key metaphorical constructs in formulating more environmentally responsive design approaches. Part III (Chapters 8–11), "Ecoarchitectural strategies and orders," considers ecologically oriented collaborative models, design processes, and ordering systems and concludes with discussion of "aqueous architectures" as paradigmatic hybrids of natural and built systems with potential to transform the expression, function, and journey of water in the city.

I direct these ideas to a next generation of designers concerned with the impact of urban growth on environmental quality. They are intended to help enable future architects to play an active and innovative role in reshaping cities. I am hopeful their powers of creative inventiveness will be sought after in a society drawn to higher levels of resourcefulness.

The rewards of teaching in a professional design program are many and include ongoing correspondence with those in the academy and in practice whose views inspire and challenge. I am indebted to my students and colleagues in the School of Architecture and Allied Arts at the University of Oregon motivated to tackle issues of environmental degradation in an urbanizing world. I am thankful to student leaders of the Ecological Design Center for their generosity and dedication. Individuals whose contributions have been most direct, those who I have worked alongside, coauthored papers with, and served on thesis committees with include: Stefan Behnisch, Frances Bronet, G.Z. Brown, Mark Cabrinha, Nancy Cheng, David Cook, Don Corner, Howard Davis, Alan Dickman, Tom DiSanto, Yianni Doulis, Stephen Duff, Michael Fifield, Tom Fowler, Corie Harlan, Joanne Hogarth, David Hulse, Bart Johnson, Mark Johnson, Ron Kellett, Peter Keyes, Alison Kwok, Kaarin Kundson, Nico Larco, Richard Leplastrier, Anna Liu, Michael Lucas, Margot McDonald, Brian Melton, Erin Moore, Tom Osdoba, Ken Radtkey, Ryan Ruggiero, Adam Sharkey, Michael Singer, Shannon (McGinley) Sinkin, Rob Thallon, Christine Theodoropoulos, Roxi Thoren, Ted Toadvine, Alex Wyndham, Jenny Young, Robert Young, and Leonard Yui. I am especially grateful to Josh Cerra; his ability to negotiate multiple disciplinary and professional terrains in both design and the natural sciences earns my deep admiration.

I wish to thank my family: Mullers, Clagetts, Corletts – pragmatic visionaries all – and in particular my wife, friend, and creative influence, Cathy Corlett. Her input has been enormous. I dedicate this book to our son Calder Eames Corlett Muller. May he grow up in a global city of natural plenty.

Introduction

All values must remain vulnerable, and those that do not are dead.[1]

But what the birds cry is what the world cries in the end.[2]

Ideas can act as forces of nature.[3]

Value-laden attitudes toward the environment at the outset of architectural investigations influence processes of design. The profession's contribution to environmental degradation through the creation of inefficient and unhealthy architectures can in part be attributed to these initial predispositions. Awareness of more diverse and encompassing conceptualizations, with primary consideration in this book on ecological theories and processes, can shift architectural practices, and consequently the resourcefulness and life-enhancing qualities of built outcomes. These premises motivate the following provocations on how dispositions influence method and what new factors might be brought into the design and creation of working ecoarchitectures.

In schools of architecture today, where one imagines a high degree of interdisciplinary outreach commensurate with the enterprise, there is enormous work to do in comprehending manners and languages of those in other fields. Architects amplify a necessary fusion of humanities and sciences: physics, tectonics, history, aesthetics, design communication, sociology, ecology, other. Emerging and unprecedented environmental challenges demand cultivation of robust new strategic interdisciplinary alliances that will redefine the contribution and constitution of the architectural profession and the manner in which projects are deployed in the urban landscape. Architectural education is poised uniquely to explore emerging models of intensive, schematic integrated practice, and in so doing make good on the ecologist and designer Alexander Felson's conviction: "Creativity of architecture could serve humanity better if architects were more aware of ecological knowledge."[4]

The destabilizing influence of ecology

> **The animal world and that of plant life are not utilized merely because they are there, but because they suggest a mode of thought.**
>
> (Claude Lévi-Strauss, *Totemism*)[5]

Sustainable architectural discourse centers on embodied energy of materials, energy efficiency, water conservation, and other aspects of building behavior that can be measured and simulated and where improvements can be gauged. A "living systems" vernacular as an important next step, where buildings and landscapes interact in mutually supporting ways, invites heightened levels of complexity and contingency; this may explain why ecological considerations have lagged behind other dimensions of green building. Ecologists, operating at a great range of spatial and temporal scales, work from multiple paradigms of how ecosystems function. Less predictable and capable of codification than other realms of architecture, ecology as a source of meaning proves unstable and foregrounds the provisional stature of knowledge. As Haila and Levins claim: "Principles derived from ecology are likely to prove transitory."[6] Climate change, urbanization, and other human-induced phenomena that accelerate the simplification and isolation of ecosystems exacerbate epistemological uncertainty.

In architecture, a gap exists between a stable ground of translatable design methodologies and a hunch that designers must remain open to the unforeseen, that the unknown and underrepresented exceed and overflow, leak from, hover above, or burrow under the totality of any system, no matter how comprehensive the conceptual framework. Such a reality is reinforced by engagement with ecological concerns. While current architectural design protocols often assume as inconsequential anything overlooked, "undiscoveries" are potentially of great import. To state a conviction of the late German architect Guenther Behnisch:

Architecture should remain open for as long as possible; it should not be isolated too soon from factors that are as yet unknown and cannot yet be known. Areas of freedom must be preserved; to give a chance to the things that fail to get the attention they deserve in our everyday lives, but still may mean more to us than those that in any case force themselves upon us.[7]

With ecological systems in mind, "things that fail to get the attention they deserve in our everyday lives" include species threatened in part by actions and unintended consequences of designers and developers. By adopting a posture of humility and embracing acts of architectural production that invite areas of freedom and allow for excess, a project acquires, as landscape architect Walter Hood encourages, a desirable "strangeness."[8]

Perhaps the most prudent approach in working with ecologies as fundamentally **open systems**, those that are continually stimulated and renewed by outside influences, is to devise systems of design and collaboration that are themselves open (openness is very different from being vague). This outlook differs from certain systems-oriented contemporary approaches to ecological architecture perpetuating a modernist quest for the all-embracing.

In the introduction to *Ecodesign*, Ken Yeang makes the case that:

It must be clear that ecodesign is still in its infancy. Humans are tampering with the biosphere, and from the devastation already inflicted and from studies by ecologists it is evident that ecosystems and their reaction to human activities are not fully understood. It is not likely that humans will understand them in the time period that they have to make decisions.[9]

Earlier, on the same page, Yeang suggests optimistically:

This manual sets out to ... provide a clear and useful definition of ecodesign, and to present a sound, comprehensive and unifying theoretical framework for a *definitive* approach and basis for ecodesign to facilitate our production of built forms and the design of their related systematic properties and functions.[10]

Yeang's endeavor to furnish a "definitive" approach to designing with ecosystems "not fully understood" speaks to a wider ambivalence amongst environmental advocates: on the one hand, recognition of the overwhelming complexity of ecology; on the other, a wish that it deliver answers about the world in full resolution. Philosopher of science Bruno Latour reflects on claims of the truth of ecology assumed by many in the environmental movement, and cautions against the "total connectivity, the global ecosystem, the catholicity that wants to embrace everything, all this is what always seems to accompany the erecting of an ecological way of thinking."[11] In the creation of a unifying umbrella, overlooked are elements and phenomena of potentially great significance.

Latour's reservations resemble those many feel about sustainable architecture as conventions and measures pertaining to it normalize. According to philosopher Helen Mallinson: "One might argue that, for all its claims to represent a new or different attitude, sustainable architecture is likely to beget a more, not less, coercive environment than that traceable in the march of modernism."[12]

"Coercion" is conformity to a narrowing set of languages and images of sustainable architecture, embedded assumptions about the primary subject of a designer's attention, and the stable submissiveness of environmental background. Latour offers the designer words of caution:

> **The human–nonhuman pair does not refer us to a distribution of beings of the pluriverse, but to an uncertainty, to a profound doubt about the nature of action, to a whole gamut of positions regarding the trials that make it possible to define an actor.**[13]

"Profound doubt" and great uncertainty need not paralyze but rather prompt exploratory, trial-like forward movement, with a view to projects as speculations on architecture's life-enhancing potential. Rather than confirming so many "givens," ecological architectures as open experiments may help designers, as I hope to demonstrate and as Latour suggests, "associate the notion of external reality with surprises and events rather than with simply 'being-there.' "[14]

Viewing nature as an actor becomes a means to imbue cultural constructs – including works of architecture – with *natural powers*.

New metaphors for green architectures

> **If the objects of the environment were only as plastic as the materials of poetic art, men would never have been obliged to have recourse to creation in the medium of words.**[15]
>
> **(John Dewey, *Human Nature and Conduct*)**

Mosaics of habitat structures, processes of riparian ecosystem formation, vegetated canopy networks, the journey of water from clouds to the river, and open, events-driven systems: ecological phenomena, biological entities, and descriptions thereof offer unlimited sources of inspiration for design: for space-making, symbolizing, and synthesizing and for calling attention to dynamic processes and temporal dimensions of architecture. Explorations in this book have as much to do with expanding the designer's creative potential, the nimbleness and richness of her vision, as with concerns over environmental quality. Both are critically important in travelling over the depths of sustainable architecture and most readily advanced in concert.

The poetic potential of greener architectures prompts consideration of the role of **metaphor** in design. More than architects care to admit, metaphors operate as formidable tools, highlighting awareness of attributes often overlooked or undervalued in the design process. Further, metaphors viewed broadly as indicators of a larger conceptual orientation, a "horizon of expectation" of cherished aesthetic and ethical commitments, encourage use of particular tools over others.[16]

Philosopher Richard Rorty offers a dramatic take on the dynamism of metaphor that relates to previous considerations of ecology and openness:

> **A metaphor is, so to speak, a voice from outside logical space, rather than an empirical filling-up of a portion of that space, or a logical-philosophical**

**clarification of the structure of that space. It is a call to change one's
language and one's life, rather than a proposal about how to systemize
either.**[17]

With a goal to advance more deeply green approaches to architecture, how
might evolving metaphorical predispositions alter a designer's range of vision as
to what is achievable? What explains growing interest among contemporary
architects in landscape-focused and ecologically derived metaphors and terms as
formative design inspiration? In what ways might architects appropriate
provocative conceptual framings emerging from landscape ecology, landscape
architecture, environmental philosophy, and ecological restoration, disciplines
that embed uncertainty in systems of knowledge production?

The emphasis in what follows will be to scrutinize understandings of ecology
and landscape as embedded in the metaphorical constructs of designers, to
entertain and put in motion hybrid conceptual drivers that may assist in aligning
the highly efficient and the fantastically earthbound, above all to summon
prospects for creating works of architecture as choreographies of urban
ecological performance.

This project is both descriptive and prescriptive; weighing in on the rhetoric of
sustainable architecture, it adds to the balance. In attempting to move between
several camps (discourses), in using fuzzy, accommodating terms that offer
designers a desirable degree of what architect Ken Radtkey would describe as
"loose precision," I open myself to criticism.[18] Perhaps offering a degree of
sophistication relative to how architects usually invoke ecology-related terms,
my treatment of these may strike an ecologist, landscape architect, or
environmental philosopher as problematic. These shortcomings may have to do
with more than terminology: natural scientists may find speculative architectural
proposals for intervening in degraded urban sites to be less than optimal relative
to the particular and exacting natures of their domains of inquiry. My goal is to
advance dialog as to how to align architecture and ecology and to welcome
critique of design prospects motivated out of environmental concern. To be
sure, designers in their creative excitement frequently borrow concepts from

science with insufficient rigor. And yet, given pressing environmental challenges and the need for disciplinary alliance, this borrowing has value: scientists can help set designers straight and at the same time inventive and informed design speculation can aid in furthering and applying ecological knowledge.

Philosophers of language have every right to debate my inclusive treatment of metaphor as both a specific linguistic utterance *and* an indicator of a larger conceptual frame. Further, my focus on metaphor may seem disproportionate relative to its significance in architecture, and I acknowledge the shortcomings of highlighting one aspect of design inquiry over others. That said, because I concentrate on the propitious formative stages of design – what dimensions enter into designers' conceptual inspirations and what consequences these have for making ecological architectures – a detailed discussion of metaphor as design provocation is warranted. Here I owe a debt to my students who, through curiosity and insight, continually generate the most striking and playfully inventive of terms.

Notes

1   Bachelard 1994, 59.
2   Williams 1973, 52.
3   Takacs 1996, 105.
4   Personal correspondence with Alexander Felson, March 1, 2011.
5   Lévi-Strauss 1963, 12.
6   Haila and Levins 1992, 7.
7   From the transcript of a lecture that Guenther Behnisch delivered at the University of Oregon School of Architecture and Allied Arts, May 1990.
8   From a lecture that Walter Hood delivered at the HOPES EcoDesign Arts Conference at the University of Oregon, April 13, 2012.
9   Yeang 2006, 24.
10   Yeang 2006, 24 (italics added).
11   Latour 2004, 22.
12   Mallinson 2004, 177.
13   Latour 2004, 73.

14 Latour 2004, 79.

15 Dewey 2002, 255–256.

16 See Gross 2010, 32.

17 Rorty 1991, 13.

18 Radtkey uses the "loose precision" to describe a proper mindset in the preliminary stages of design, where priority is placed on inclusiveness of possibility. I worked beside Ken Radtkey for seven years. This is one of his many memorable and apt figures of speech.

Part I

Ecological Architectures within a Broader Context

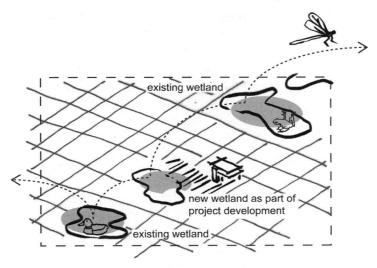

A project as a stepping-stone supporting species movement in an urban
landscape.

**One simply cannot overemphasize the key role of problem formulation in
seeking cooperation and success in environmental management. And at the
heart of problem formulation is the question of how we talk about – how we
articulate and discuss – environmental problems.[5]**

An ecoarchitecture as a form of "critical" political ecology relies on the ability
of a project team "to reveal the hidden politics within supposedly neutral
statements about ecological causality."[6] The conceptualization of a work of
architecture is at once the gathering of the best available information, the
space of dialog, and an accounting of responsibility. A realized work of
architecture testifies to the process and breadth of environmental
consideration; it is the outcome of the non-neutral set of approvals, contracts,
simulations, and representations that optimally pertain to resource efficiency
as well as to how a project functions as an alteration of dynamic (eco)systems
over time.

Organizers of conferences, symposia, and summits dedicated to advancing green strategies for designing built environments frequently portray climate change as *the* environmental problem, one that, due to its severity, trumps all other issues.[7] While climate change is the monster in the bestiary, a monumental threat demanding immediate and aggressive response on the part of architects and society at large, other environmental issues deserve the designer's attention. "Simultaneous stressors" include diminished air and water quality and a downward spiral of habitat fragmentation and consequent loss of biodiversity. Ecosystem degradation and simplification account for the mass extinction now underway, the sixth in the history of the world and the first precipitated by a species. The political scientist Stephen Meyer offers a sobering description of the momentum of this event: "The average rate of extinction over the past hundred million years has hovered at several species per year. Today the extinction rate surpasses 3,000 species per year and is accelerating rapidly."[8]

By helping stem the worst of climate change *and* other grave environmental problems such as the degradation of habitat necessary to species survival, designers can contribute to a future where a plenitude of beings populate the world and dreams of our children. The extent and nature of alteration of habitat conditions in the decades ahead will serve as a particularly telling measure of collective awareness, concerted desire, and sense of restraint that enables specialists – special beings – to thrive. Architects and other design professionals can make critical contributions to this effort by virtue of the projects they take on and the design processes they embrace.

Bryan Norton argues:

> **Changes in natural systems attendant upon human population and technological expansion represent a series of more and more irreversible experiments in reducing the complexity and diversity of the plant life and cultural practices. Natural systems, as well as conventional cultural practices, are undergoing constant "disturbance" at every level and on every scale. What we need is a new way of talking about and evaluating rapid, often irreversible changes that will result from continued economic and technological growth.[9]**

Urbanism and architectural development are exemplar forms of economic and technological growth that will shape the scope of irreversible change in the decades ahead. Until recently, the city has been examined as a concentrator and facilitator of economic, social, political, and spiritual activities, less so an entity influencing and responding to, let alone abetting, ecological processes. Today, more and more people act under the conviction that urban environments are unique settings for ecological possibility that can do more than serve as sacrifice zones for desirable specialist species and breeding grounds for pests.

Population biologist Michael Rosenzweig makes the case that, if it is assumed human dominated landscapes such as cities are largely incapable of supporting native habitat populations, and accounting for basic biological "rules" such as species/area relationships as well as rates of urbanization and land use change, we are simply running out of space. Natural areas such as wildlife refuges, harboring the "inherited diversity" of remnant and isolated populations, will become so compromised that "there will be no immigration rate to supplement whatever meager speciation rate we still have."[10] Rosenzweig calculates a loss of up to 95 percent of the world's species during this mass extinction (other studies offer less sobering assessments, with extinction rates often varying between 20 and 50 percent).

Viewing urbanized areas as capable of accommodating significant nonhuman populations, the situation may not be so dire. This will require a different and vastly more inclusive way of structuring our conurbations, new "regimes" that alter the metabolism of the city. As landscape architectural educator and theorist Bart Johnson suggests, we are only now developing frameworks to "harness hard urban systems," the very systems seen as primary contributors to ecological degradation, as one locus for habitat regeneration.[11] Meyer believes "harnessing" every available landscape – urban or otherwise – is essential in preventing further species loss during processes of reestablishment of broader ecological networks. The city must act as one component in a comprehensive interim strategy to "maintain viable source populations of still-plentiful relicts for the next 100 years as we try to put in place larger-scale landscape protection."[12] This is especially important and daunting in the context of climate change that exacerbates habitat degradation and species extinctions and constrains the ability of organisms to adapt. While during previous climate shifts species' "survival was insured to a large extent by dispersal across the landscape," patterns of development have subsequently closed off avenues for dispersal.[13] Contemporary approaches to urbanism and urbanization must account for patterns of "dispersability" in this transforming climatic context.

Additional factors suggest the importance of the city and urbanizing areas as bound to prospects for ecological regeneration. Cities in North America and throughout the world were settled and developed in areas of high biological value, for example along riparian corridors so critical to economic expansion. Recent urban ecological research, such as that produced through the Long Term Ecological Research project (LTER), indicate that urban environments harbor higher levels of biodiversity than commonly thought, in some cases more than on agricultural and other rural lands.[14] This is so in part because certain activities located on urban fringes and rural hinterlands that have been shown to be detrimental to health are not acceptable in (urban) landscapes with large concentrations of human populations (for instance, the spraying of crops with pesticides).[15]

Given that so many urban sites have been compromised due to the predominance of economic activities that have simplified biological systems, the potential exists for urban redevelopment to improve circumstances dramatically, in both places of high visibility and in those "forgotten" parts of the city ripe for revitalization and newfound presence. Particularly promising are those challenging urban conditions where the grid confronts marked topographical change or otherwise "unruly" physical circumstance such as a creek, outcrop, mesa, or wetland. Often these features have been disturbed and transformed into low-value human uses such as log ponds, gravel operations, storage facilities, landfills, and junkyards: the collective legacy of the makeshift. Given their latent potential to accommodate the "pluriverse of multinaturals" that Bruno Latour celebrates, that is, overlapping associations of living systems that people can help set in motion,[16] the marginalized condition becomes a newly visible feature in the emerging city, a nexus of intensified social, economic,

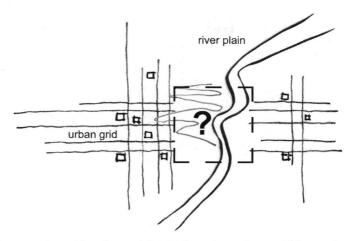

river plain

urban grid

?

Between urban grids and natural features lie neglect and potential for greatly enhanced human and natural systems productivity.

recreational, and biological uses, a critical piece in the making of urban ecological fabric.

Even a constrained urban site not linked optimally to larger, functioning ecological networks has potential to contribute to improved biophysical processes. "Ecodesigner" and architect Ken Yeang speculates as to "ecological processes that exceed their spatial extent."[17] The landscape ecologist Richard Foreman challenges us to better understand and work with "site ecologies," the dynamics that operate or could operate locally: "Site ecology, or the ecology of small spaces, needs to have a much higher profile, especially in design."[18] He further contends:

> The major components of a rigorous or small-space ecology exist, but are scattered over several fields. A great opportunity beckons for someone to make the synthesis. It will become a leg of the future design and planning fields.[19]

If a site is isolated and surrounded by impervious tarmacs, it is still possible for it to harbor, as Josh Cerra puts it, "symbolic ecologies" – island-like vegetated habitat structures that offer didactic value and other potential benefits.[20] Adopting an optimistic posture, it is hoped those responsible for subsequent developments on neighboring sites will take a cue from these symbols, recognize their functional potential, and introduce vegetative structures, perhaps coupled closely with architectural elements in dense urban settings, that link to the "symbolic" site and those beyond. Neighborhoods or municipalities might then advocate that subsequent projects incorporate connective landscape structures that the individual catalytic projects anticipated. Ideally and over time small-space ecologies and broad-scale landscape systems operate in mutual support.

Introducing symbolic ecologies and attending to the marginalized yet biologically valuable spaces of the city: such efforts do *not* represent an attempt to return to an uncompromised "state of nature." Landscapes throughout North America have been managed actively for millennia, making nostalgic retreat indefensible philosophically and impossible practically. And for the majority of urban sites, human activity will continue to dominate. This endeavor rather speaks to an awareness of past processes and conditions (pertaining to habitat formation, capacity for dispersal, etc.) that can most positively anticipate trajectories from the present day forward. Such an approach represents a hope of a *future of differential possibility*, where biodiversity corresponds directly to evolutionary potential. Environmental philosopher David Wood maintains:

> From an evolutionary point of view, we are witnessing a massive loss of differentiation. And with the loss of this difference we are losing the possibilities of further transformation. Every species that dies out is the loss of an adventure with the future, and with such loss of differentiation we also lose ecological complexity, and hence the diminution of constitutional relationality in nature. What this points to is not mourning for a lost purity, a privileged identity, but rather for a lost wealth of differential possibility.[21]

This view of loss, difference, and future expands the designer's perspective and scope: how is it possible to generate radically more productive urban environments from the standpoint of human need *and* biological diversity?

What strategies constitute a process of "filling in" gaps of developable land in our cities (a form of growth intended to counter sprawl) while "fitting out" these very sites in such a way that they support ecological services? What are the means to reconcile the tensions manifest in James Evans' recognition that we are placing "spatial demands on cities to deliver increasingly developed landscapes while simultaneously becoming more sustainable?"[22]

Cities typically function as "highly ordered dissipative structures" within complex, global, biophysical processes.[23] In order to counteract entropic tendencies and meet new spatial demands, designers are called upon to embrace a process of **collapsing** natural functions together with those of human-driven patterning, a "stacking of value" in increasingly dense contexts. "Stacking value" is the skill of the designer in identifying synergies between elements and uses and deploying the minimum number of design moves to greatest possible effect, such that function and inhabitability overflow a space's size. Although site-scale architectural interventions provide the focus in what follows, urban ecological design as functional and spatial collapsing and stacking must occur at multiple scales: public transit corridors with properly configured rights-of-way can double as corridors that facilitate wildlife crossings (a transit nexus becomes an ecological nexus); urban alleyways can become sites for transmission of water, power, cyclists, social ferment, native birds, and pollinators; buildings can frame and furnish niches and other habitat structures for a variety of species. Ecological design is informed, resourcefully minded, radically intensified place-making for a multiplicity of lifestyles and life histories.

Notes

1   Wood 2005, 173.
2   Foreman 2004, 24.
3   Fraker 1984, 104 (italics added)
4   The California Integrated Management Waste Board's efforts to decrease the amount of material entering the state's waste stream makes particularly palpable the problem of construction demolition debris. See: www. calrecycle.ca.gov/condemo/pubs.htm for a list of publications related to

this topic, including *Designing with Vision: A Technical Manual for Material Choices in Sustainable Construction.*

5   Norton 2005, xi.

6   Forsyth 2003, 53.

7   The description of the Pennsylvania State University Department of Architecture Committee for Environmentally Conscious Architecture's (CECA) Symposium "Environmentally Conscious Architecture – Educating Future Architects," October 23–25, 2009 offers but one example of this emphasis (this is not a criticism of an excellent symposium).

8   Meyer 2006, 3–4.

9   Norton 2005, 199.

10 Rosenzweig 2003, 136.

11 Personal correspondence with Bart Johnson, May 30, 2008.

12 Meyer 2006, 87–88.

13 Meyer 2006, 30.

14 See for example Pickett *et al.*, 2008.

15 See Coolidge 2000. This book traces Route 58, an outermost rung of the Los Angeles megalopolis along which "marginal" activities are located: weapons-testing sites, power plants, monoculture agriculture, feedlots, etc.

16 See Latour 2004.

17 Yeang 2006, 41.

18 Forman 2002, 90.

19 Forman 2002, 90.

20 I partnered with Josh Cerra teaching architecture studios for five years and "symbolic ecologies" was a term he used frequently.

21 Wood 2005, 185.

22 Evans 2007, 132.

23 Rees and Wackernagel 2008 24.

CHAPTER 2

Commons

Privately owned land and developments can play important roles in elevating ecological performance of the metropolis. By strengthening corridor connectivity and incorporating habitat structures and ancillary pockets they can, according to Josh Cerra, "augment publicly held open spaces that function as the backbone of working landscape ecologies in urban contexts."[1] Development pressures in Oregon's Willamette Valley speak more broadly to the challenge of maintaining and building ecological integrity in urbanizing landscapes. Over 95 percent of the land in the valley, the most populous and rapidly urbanizing part of the state, is privately owned, severely limiting opportunities for public conservation and rehabilitation of native ecosystems. In discussing the restoration of its increasingly rare native habitats, Bruce Campbell contends: "Conservation strategies need to focus on restoring and maintaining more natural ecosystem processes and functions within landscapes that are managed primarily for other values," that is, values generally associated with economic livelihood on lands under private ownership.[2]

While ecological conservation and restoration projects are undertaken in many kinds of ecosystems at many scales, involving public or private lands or a combination, natural scientists and environmental stewards focus increasingly on the "typical," that is, the Jeffersonian, democratic, small-scale urban lot, and the impact of site-scale development on a broader landscape ecological matrix. While private lots set arbitrary borders relative to historical processes of ecosystem formation and species distribution, their march across the landscape establishes new regimes with distinct energy and nutrient flows and population dynamics that urban ecologists endeavor to understand (using the same frameworks they use for more "natural" systems). Landscape architectural scholar Joan Iverson Nassauer frames persuasively how long-term environmental quality will be the sum of ecological understandings of and decisions made at the scale of the individual landholding:

We must work at this democratic scale of ownership, the single lot or the single farm or ranch, to achieve ecological health beyond public lands and beyond the anomalies of privileged and enlightened land development. In the United States, where recent legal decisions have tended to narrowly interpret public interests in limiting private-property rights, and where strong cultural traditions favor the rights of landowners to do what they deem most suitable on their land, overall ecological health depends on the aggregation of innumerable individual landowner's decisions.[3]

Greater focus on the ecological significance of privately held lands corresponds to growing awareness of the inadequacy of public investment in environmental protection. Meyer's finding that "annual global spending on ecosystem protection (including acquisition) is just over $3 billion (the price of two B-2 bombers)" brings urgency to the reality that significant improvements in urban, regional, and word-wide ecological health will not come about exclusively through public policy and spending.[4] So do the many bond measures that are passed that enable public agencies in cities and urbanized regions to acquire properties for purposes of conservation, yet only allow purchase of a small percentage of lands deemed critical for continued habitat function and other important ecological processes.

As part of a broader effort to restore and protect natural assets, the Nature in Neighborhoods Program at Metro (Portland, Oregon's regional planning authority) led a process of citizen engagement and mapping to identify "Habitat Conservation Areas" (HCAs) throughout the metropolitan region.[5] The majority of HCAs – riparian corridors, wetland complexes, upland woodlands, and other features of significant ecological value – fall on privately held lands. Perhaps given their value and collective potential to safeguard and support critical urban ecological services, these areas should be spared from development. And yet, as Metro recognizes, a no-development stance fails to account for the rights and economic stakes of private landowners. Further, given population growth projections for the region, forbidding development on urban lands containing HCAs will add to the pressure to expand Portland's urban growth boundary and likely result in development of high-quality open spaces in urban hinterlands.

In response to these circumstances, Metro utilized HCA overlays to introduce its highly progressive, incentive-oriented Title XIII "Nature in Neighborhoods" habitat-based development ordinance (2009).[6] Under this policy, if a developer/ design team identifies an HCA occupying a portion of the site they wish to invest in and build upon, and they devise a plan that avoids construction within the HCA and that provides appropriate buffer, they are awarded density bonuses as well as relaxation of property line setbacks, building height restrictions and parking requirements for the remainder of the site, along with other benefits. Metro is encouraging through private development a morphological transformation of the urban environment characterized by smaller building footprints and taller buildings, intact habitat features at the site scale, and a metro-scale network of connected greenways and riparian corridors.

This innovative example points to the importance of aligning innovative design approaches, policy instruments, regulatory frameworks, and financial mechanisms in encouraging ecologically minded entrepreneurship and development. In this regard, it is worth speculating about the potential interplay of San Diego architect Teddy Cruz's "microurbanistic" approach to block-scale urban redevelopment in support of disenfranchised communities and involving nonprofits, activists, and other nontraditional developer clients (what Cruz envisions will be a prevalent form of future development in American cities), and the emerging "EcoDistricts" initiative in which innovative, public/private investments finance neighborhood upgrades such as the installation of "green streets" and other forms of sustainable infrastructure. Cruz works to promote small-scale, "patchwork" urban design involving high levels of community engagement.[7] EcoDistricts endeavor to accelerate neighborhood and district-scale innovations in sustainability, with a focus on "performance areas" that include: community vitality; air quality and carbon; energy; access and mobility; water, habitat, and ecosystem function; and materials management.[8] Together, these efforts prompt new and enabling patterns of urbanism, durable and ecologically functional systems that anticipate and support piecemeal incremental growth.

Interest in environmental futures as a vehicle for speculative urban development leads to ideas of expanding ecosystems markets to the city. Instruments that address climate stabilization, hydrological regulation, and biological diversity benefits focus typically on impacts of economically driven activity in places that are relatively intact ecologically, for example a forested landscape that includes old growth and other natural assets in its matrix.[9] Application of these tools in an urban redevelopment scenario would concentrate on both the vibrancy of local urban districts and the quality of urban ecosystems. Such instruments would incentivize optimization of site-scale performance as part of a larger endeavor to pool and distribute ecosystem resources and services. My site lies low and is optimal for collecting water; your (neighboring) site has excellent solar access. If I can borrow your "sun" (in the form of solar energy) as an outcome of development and/or retrofit of your site, I will treat your stormwater as an outcome of mine.

This approach to ecological urbanism, stimulating economic behavior while building community capacity, may prove ultimately more transformative than the current emphasis on net zero buildings, that, although commendable, represents a form of loner sustainability that fails to capitalize on synergies, proximity, and access that are fundamental to the nature of the city. In a capacity-building exercise, opportunities exist for emerging architects with a combination of design and management skills and high degrees of ecological literacy to act as broker restorationists who artfully arrange transactions between sites and neighborhoods; even smaller-scale commissions can yield region-scale biological dividends.

If ecological considerations point to the importance of private development, and if partnerships of lots and blocks promise greatly improved urban performance, ecology is also a design cue for negotiating space at the project scale and for making "compact" forms of growth more palatable. A vision for redevelopment of a typical city block in a post-war residential neighborhood might treat as one interrelated problem increased density and improved ecological performance through coordinated stormwater management and reintroduction of woodland habitat, superimposed threads of green extending across lots and connecting nearby urban open spaces, reestablishing paths of movement for threatened species. A landscape ecological structure (corridor) situates dwellings in a supportive context; building masses are deployed to generate a micro-ecological patterning of landscape rooms.[10] If block-sized, renaturalized "green development nodes" take root and expand to include large portions of urban land, cities can become robust participants in a comprehensive biodiversity agenda.

Village Homes in Davis, California, a 1970s-era development considered a "high risk" investment due to the compactness of dwellings and lots in comparison with more typical subdivisions, offers a compelling suburban-scale example of the stacked value of shared ecological amenity.[11] A system of copses and alleyways provides shade and access to dwellings. Homes open to small yards fronting bioswale commons and paths that form a contiguous network. In this project, the social diagram, a basic spatial organizational strategy for how people relate to and interact with one another, and the ecological diagram, a basic spatial organizational strategy for how a project treats stormwater and supports habitat, work together to elevate individual dwelling and overall community identity and fortify links between the development and its neighbors. Village Homes has sustained enormous popularity as inhabitants recognize the social and environmental benefits, and long-term investment stability, of homes situated within and organized by connective green space.

Blackbird Architects' winning entry for the Great Central Valley "Housing the Next Ten Million" competition builds from a similar organizational logic. Their "Green Archipelago" redevelopment proposal for one square mile of largely vacant land within the Bakersfield, California, city limits incorporates orchard paths that link small dwellings to a network of shallow tule lakes.[12] These lakes collect stormwater, provide a recreational amenity, and function as neighborhood landmarks; they anticipate a more ecologically functional future by recalling the waterscapes – marshes, sloughs, and peat islands – that once prevailed in this arid landscape.

In support of the commons in an urbanizing context, a relevant design challenge pertains to the translation of the synergistic spatial logic of Village Homes and green archipelagoes to projects of denser configuration. Incorporation of

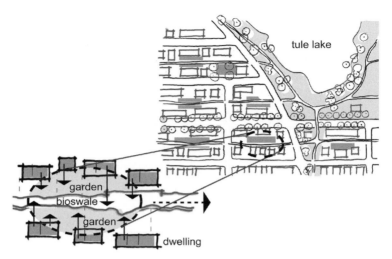

From the scale of urban districts to developments on lots, *the social diagram and the ecological diagram coincide.*

vegetated corridors, slots, patches, and other landscape structures as part of the planning of compact dwelling units in multi-story projects can contribute to an atmosphere of generosity and openness, precisely through their borrowing of the landscape. Unconditioned circulation spines such as shared stairwells in association with vegetated façades might direct and hold water, buffer dwelling units from temperature extremes, precondition air before it enters interior spaces, and provide purchases for nests (similarly, following the example of architect Hans Scharoun, corners of buildings become spatial amplifiers, orientation devices, and light-filled commons). Taking cues from projects such as Jean Renaudie and Renee Gailhoustet's housing in Ivry-sur-Seine (1969–1975), emplacement of micro-common gardens is a means to negotiate, intensify, and multiply space in support of the life between buildings and the imaginaries of those who dwell there.[13]

Within the box-like volume of Adolf Loos' (1870–1933) Kärtner Bar or American Bar in Vienna (1908), one finds three-sided booths, each with a small, lozenge-shaped table in the center. The tables are lit from below (they are light tables).

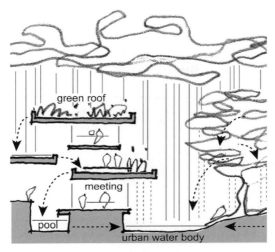

The social diagram and the ecological diagram coincide (#2): deceleration and filtration of stormwater in a forested landscape informs architectural-scale staggering of space.

Mirrors on upper portions of surrounding walls extend to the coffered, marble ceiling. In a relatively dark interior space, one gathers with one's loved one or friends around the warm focal glow of the table, not unlike a campfire, and gazes upward to an endless nighttime horizon of smoky marble sky. Loos takes a small, simple or "neutral" volume and shapes it simultaneously into immediate intimacy and endless cosmic extension. In a contemporary urban context of environmental concern, it is possible to retain Loos' paradigm of thought, invert his proposition, deploy it outwardly, and expand the palette by using what is there and what might return (birds). Working with dense formations of buildings, architects are charged with contriving a cubist plurality of space in support of a multifaceted reality.

Iris Marion Young argues that justice in society is not an exclusive matter of the distribution of rights and goods; it also pertains to relations that obtain between members and parts, the quality of those relations, and the desirability of a space of surplus (physical and conceptual) that accommodates difference.[14] Following

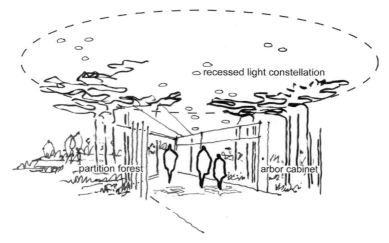

recessed light constellation

partition forest

arbor cabinet

Compact interior spaces that borrow the landscape acquire visual and psychological generosity.

from this argument, in a double move away from elitism associated deeply with histories of architecture and environmentalism, informed architects skilled at the manipulation of space can view their work as a form of urban ecological justice. Landscape architect Randolph Hester embraces an ecologically democratic design approach that endeavors to ensure people *access* to a shared public life, clean water, clean air, shelter, healthy food, green space, and functioning natural systems.[15] As part of this process, Hester encourages the placing of habitat structures in community design projects, often small overlooked spaces that through their configuration and strategic location within a broader geography can impact significantly the ability of species to flourish. Participants in the process are often in sympathy with and link strengthening of community identity with these efforts.

For Hester, innovative and ecologically democratic design is the reimagining of sites that appear oversaturated with competing expectations, where a development might at first seem to improve living standards only at the expense of shared amenities and critical habitat. To work toward "a community for all" is to acknowledge spatial specificities of multiple needs, find creative opportunity in sources of conflict, and endeavor to move beyond choice between priorities toward synthesizing them (or least cultivating a relationship with tensions that exist). For Hester, ecological design is also quite specifically the architect's commitment to utilizing inventiveness and power to transform environments in order to save a species.

To engage in an ecoarchitectural operation as a form of ethical practice is also to partake in critical self-reflection on the "logic" of sustainable architecture to which one subscribes, that is, one's attitude about the role of and dependence on technology at the nexus of spatial quality, material support, and environmental responsiveness. In their influential article "Reinterpreting Sustainable Architecture: The Place of Technology," Guy and Farmer present a range of logics that operate under the broad header of sustainable architecture, from – on one extreme – a highly sophisticated "eco-technic" (techno-rational) logic as embraced by the likes of the architect Sir Richard Rogers (high-performance green buildings made of aluminum and the latest in glazing technology), to a metaphysically holistic, eco-centric attitude toward building materials and assemblies (dwellings made from aluminum cans, recycled tires, manure, and straw).[16] Steven Moore situates this critical political ecology of a sustainable architecture within a broader consideration of a project as a set of "eco-social-technical operations" in which the architect carefully reconciles goals of environmental quality, capacity of society to embrace change (and capacity of a project to encourage it), and informed combinations of emerging technologies and those proven.[17] A less spatially impoverished, more materially economical definition of affluence and a primary goal of engendering life suggest a hybrid sustainable logic, one that assimilates light and passive solutions to environmental control, selectively smart devices of environmental awareness, and densely formed and richly open spatial organizations supportive of diverse habitat structure. Architecture as a "continuity of singularities," an idea that will be pursued in Chapter 10, is a thoughtful assemblage of disintegrated/integrated elements with direct and indirect environmental impact.

Bruno Latour links the future of democracy itself to a collective ability to decelerate the proliferation of destructive "nature–culture hybrids." For Latour, modern societies are those that separate out in discourse entities they attribute to the realm of nature and those associated with the realm of culture (think of the "outdoors" and the "business" sections of the local newspaper as one instance of this dichotomization: nature is the domain of science; culture that of politics). It is this very theoretical polarization that permits undesirable "nature/ cultures" to proliferate in troubling ways – for example, climate change and nuclear waste. Latour scrutinizes how we constitute, transform, and continually reevaluate these hybrid human–nonhuman assemblages. He calls for more democratic participation in moderating and modulating these: "The production of hybrids, by becoming explicit and collective, becomes the object of an enlarged democracy that regulates or slows down its cadence."[18] Through the choices they make, the collaborations they encourage and the ways projects intervene in and affect ecological systems, teams of designers, engineers, and natural scientists can help legislate a more openly democratic cadence. Architectural design is very much the politics of nature.

Designers, developers, and ecologists can help establish more outwardly oriented, inclusive patterns of residency by honoring fluidly mobile dimensions of human dwelling, where "homebound" is temporary stasis amidst daily and annual rounds, the flux-like lateral spread of comings and goings. Philosopher Michel Serres warns of the myopia of people forever indoors and the implications of architectures as fortification building: "We've even walled up the windows in order to hear one another better or argue more easily. We communicate irrepressibly. We busy ourselves only with our own networks."[19] John Dewey's birdlike metaphor of human activity as an "alternation of flights and perchings" suggests a more comprehensive view,[20] as does Karsten Harries' claim that "we cannot really be at home in the world as long as we fail to accept that we are wayfarers, nowhere fully at home."[21]

If wandering is indeed a dimension of the fullness of dwelling, if, to quote William Kittredge, "surely as any river, we exist in movement," the architect responsible for the "immediate space" of site development is led to pay greater attention to the impacts of an ever-expanding domesticity, a home economics that has extended to all folds, niches, and steppes of the globe.[22] In his book

Cultures of Habitat, naturalist Gary Paul Nabhan observes a correlation in the United States between degree of movement and instability of a human population, as measured by the number of in- and out-migrations per capita per county per year, and the instability of nonhuman population, as measured by the number of species in decline per county.[23] This consequence makes imperative the need to structure human-dominated landscapes – relationships between streets, trail and transit systems, open spaces, infrastructures, and buildings – in a manner that accommodates the complex, open patterning of wandering and dwelling of numerous beings. Compact and resourceful site-scale projects become conceptualized as explicit and critical intersection points, stopovers, and in other ways partial fulfillments of these encompassing systems.

Kerry Whiteside suggests: "Civility designates our ability to invoke nature freely and unpredictably, by moving among the symbolic registers of identity, convention, and science."[24] If lack of natural simplicity is an accustomed dimension of cosmopolitanism, a sophisticated contemporary urban architecture assists in the (re)generation of excessive natural complexity. If now, according to Stilgoe, "an increasingly urban population fears any intimacy with uncontrolled nature, especially darkness," cities as natures of free invocation follow upon a conception of architectural developments not as ever-more systems inputs in an unending process of compartmentalization but rather as the sustenance of the uncommon and a rewilding of the commons.[25]

Notes

1 Personal correspondence.
2 Campbell 2004, 3.
3 Nassauer 1997, 71.
4 Meyer 2006, 86.
5 See: www.oregonmetro.gov.
6 Nature in Neighborhoods' 2009 "Integrating Habitats" competition explores habitat-friendly design opportunities associated with this strategy; for descriptions of the competition goals and results see: www. oregonmetro.gov/index.cfm/go/by.web/id=21627.

7   For an illustration of Cruz' "Casa Familiar: Living Rooms at the Border" project in San Ysidro, California, see Princeton Architectural Press. 2002.

8   For an overview of EcoDistricts as promoted by the Portland Sustainability Institute (PoSI), see: www.pdxinstitute.org/index.php/ecodistricts.

9   See for example www.ecosystemmarketplace.com.

10 See "Street and House" in Habraken 1998, 164–169; now add the dimension of ecology.

11 For a description of Village Homes, see: www.villagehomesdavis.org/.

12 Tule lakes are shallow, marsh-like water bodies that were found throughout the Central Valley prior to urbanization and the conversion of lands to agricultural use.

13 See Scalbert 2004.

14 See Young 1990.

15 See Hester 2006.

16 Guy and Farmer 2001.

17 See Moore and Wilson 2009.

18 Latour 1993, 41.

19 Serres 1992, 29.

20 Dewey 2002, 179.

21 Harries 1998, 166.

22 Kittredge 2000, 138.

23 See Nabhan 1997, 1–2. Investigations into the ecological context of the American West, where Gary Paul Nabhan dwells, led to identification of two interrelated factors: (1) movement/migration has been a distinguishing characteristic of cultural identity amongst native North American peoples (see Calloway 2003, 53: "Movement was often an important part of the process by which groups became 'a people' ") and (2): perhaps more than anywhere else on earth, variability, unpredictability, and sudden change are key factors in understanding North America's unruly climatic history (see, for example, Flannery 2001).

24 Whiteside 2002, 181.

25 Stilgoe 2003, 20.

CHAPTER 3

Ecosystem Models

Architects attend with increasing sophistication to ecological concerns in the design process and the manner in which projects are situated in and interact with the surrounding landscape. And yet despite this hopeful endeavor to bind buildings to life in the sky, canopy, and ground, architects, no matter how pragmatic or specific their approach to urban ecological design, rely necessarily on abstractions as to how ecosystems function and how humans most constructively interact with them. These prevailing modes of conceptualization relate to broader cultural reliance on what political ecologist Tim Forsyth describes as environmental "orthodoxies."[1] Uncritical acceptance of these limits the ability of architects to produce transformative work.

Haila and Levins make evident that ecologists themselves, not just designers looking to ecology as a source of meaning and inspiration, often overlook underlying models and motivations in pursuing their work:

> **Whether ecologists find stability or productivity or diversity or adaptability the interesting characteristic of ecosystems will certainly influence the course of their research. But the reasons for such choices, as distinct from arguments for them, are rarely examined.[2]**

An incomplete list of determinants and key characteristics used to describe ecological systems include web, balance, drift, resilience, stability, disturbance, succession, climax, dominant, emergent, continuity, community, refrain, event, open, feedback, mosaic, matrix, dynamic, neutral, equilibrium, and non-equilibrium. These summarizations of underlying "natures" – what Taleb would caution as "the dangerous compression of narratives" – have great consequence for the nuance and comprehensiveness of articulating environmental problems and evaluating effectiveness of interventions over time.[3] The inadequacy of any one construct, given the complexity and vastness involved, suggests the value of examining a limited number of models of ecosystems and the ways they motivate architectural inquiry.

Equilibrium models of ecosystems

It is common for well-intentioned, green-minded students of architecture to describe as primary design motivation the minimization of project impact on a site so as to preserve a precarious natural balance. A remarkable aspect of this conviction is that in so many cases the sites in question have been degraded significantly due to previous human activity. If a site has little (remaining) ecological integrity, and suffers from biological impoverishment, why propose a "benign" intervention?

This outlook stems from an environmental "orthodoxy" that healthy ecosystems are in equilibrium and characterized by balance, stability, and homeostasis. Hubbell relates this "mainstream view" to a "*niche-assembly* perspective" that maintains:

> **Communities are groups of interacting species whose presence or absence and even their relative abundance can be deduced from "assembly rules" that are based on the ecological niches or functional roles of each species. According to this view, species coexist in interactive equilibrium with other species in the community.[4]**

Along with students of architecture, numerous "green" designers and their collaborators appeal to the notion of equilibrium as central to a properly environmental orientation. The notion of "restorative practices," for instance, foregrounds the importance of returning ecosystems to previous, preferred, and steady states. "Sustainability," the need to sustain certain processes and resources necessary to the life quality of future generations, implies a definable baseline that all can agree has to be met. Popular terms such as "checks and balances" and "web of life" correspond to this perspective as well.

The equilibrium view has deep historical roots. Sharon Kingsland argues:

> **This idea of a balance in nature was commonly accepted by natural historians well before Darwin. Forbes integrated this traditional belief, which harkened back to an earlier teleological view of nature as harmoniously regulated for the benefit of all in accordance with divine wisdom, with the new theoretical writing on evolution.[5]**

Even an influential leader in "ecodesign" theory and practice such as Ken Yeang, in attempting to embed design interventions within surrounding ecologies, unwittingly bases recommended practices on the presumption of some level of balance-like completeness. While Yeang recognizes that "ecosystems are ... dynamic systems and are always changing and in a state of flux," he also speaks of the overarching objective of ecodesign as that of "benign environmental integration," as "within each ecosystem, then, are the organisms making up the living community in balance with their environment."[6]

Certain assumptions underpin the equilibrium view. To begin, nature's balance as found in ecosystems requires respect, cautious regard, and, when necessary, the commitment of restoration. Implicit is the assumption that balance requires participation of all constituent ecosystem components, with removal of any one imperiling the system. Additionally, human activities usually have the effect of disrupting this balance with negative consequences. Humans enter the system clumsily, or worse, violently, from outside.[7] It would be preferable to disengage human and natural systems to allow optimal, unimpeded ecosystem function. The greenest design proposal is one that assumes a very small footprint so as not to upset the natural balance.

The equilibrium view poses conceptual and operational challenges. First, how does one define a balanced state? *When* did balance best characterize the ecosystem in question and how do species in combination with nonorganic elements interact to maintain it? Can people reintroduce a proper mix of species, reinstate certain functions, and expect stable relationships to (re)form and the system to act as before? Do necessary connections fall into place?

(These questions are not only daunting; for some they are misdirected. For example, O'Neill *et al.* maintain: "The old imagery of the natural world as having everything connected to everything else is shortsighted. It is the relative disconnection that constitutes the organization of the system."[8])

The ideal of nature untouched complicates and suspends constructive human engagement in ecological systems, at a time calling for new depths of exploration of forms and processes of intervention. Ironically, lack of indication of a fruitful course of action parallels conviction that an equilibrium view offers an adequately comprehensive understanding of "biophysical reality." Political ecologist Tim Forsyth challenges this:

> **Environmental explanations based on universal statements of causality and concepts of equilibrium and a teleological progression to climax are highly problematic. The explanations are problematic because they impose visions of order and predictability upon complex biophysical processes and diverse evaluations of environment that say more about the social practice of making science than the ability to know and explain biophysical reality in its totality.[9]**

Most designers have an inkling of the inadequacy of an equilibrium view – that the model has utility in observing certain kinds of conditions, yet is limiting given its persistent influence, the kinds of conclusions drawn from it, and the magnitude and compounding nature of ecological degradation. It is more valuable – and less harmful – to abandon residual views of universality and to give standing to the idea that systems do not necessarily evolve, undergo succession, and stabilize consistently and predictably. Instead, disturbances of differing magnitudes are commonplace and impact trajectories of ecosystems in profound and profoundly different ways.[10]

Non-equilibrium model of ecosystems

Disturbances as outside influences, some more common and others highly sporadic, shape ecological dynamics to the point where ecosystems might be characterized as fundamentally "open" and non-equilibrium in nature.[11] Pickett and White maintain, "The key processes common to all disturbances are alterations of resource availability and systems structure."[12] A disturbance accelerates biophysical processes as it "increases resource availability through decreased use of resources or increased decomposition or both."[13]

In discussing forest ecosystems, Fred Swanson at the Pacific Northwest Research Station of the USDA Forest Service summarizes the role of windstorms, floods, and fires as "knocking nature around."[14] Environmental forces release sequestered sources of energy and catalysts of growth such as light, water, and nutrients. A visit to a forest ecosystem allows us to behold ongoing processes of renewal instigated by tumultuous events that occurred in the past. Ecosystem heterogeneity depends on these events:

> Because disturbances occur at irregular intervals and affect areas of varied sizes, and because recolonization will be affected by random factors of dispersal, the result will be a harlequin environment varying in species makeup across space and time.[15]

Some ecologists suggest intermediate levels of disturbance versus very minor or catastrophically large disturbances can have the most positive impact on ecosystem function.[16] No matter the scale of disturbance, a non-equilibrium view directs attention to boundary conditions, transactions, and the constructive capacity of disruption. According to Holling:

> Instability, in the sense of large fluctuations, may introduce resilience and a capacity to resist. It points out the very different view of the world that can be obtained if we concentrate on the boundaries to the domain of attraction rather than on equilibrium states.[17]

A compelling dimension of working with a non-equilibrium model in design is that it requires both a nuanced and an aggressive stance with regard to the intersection of human activity and environmental quality, that architect/ landscape architect/ecologist teams focus more intently on compatibilities between building and landscape dynamics and hybrid processes that are set in motion. How might a work of architecture, both during construction and throughout its life, participate in and respond to evolving ecological conditions? What are project goals? To rehabilitate a site and catalyze transformation of its surroundings? Mediate? Replenish? Make available sequestered resources? Maximize adaptive capacity? Set in motion a series of biophysical processes? Serve as a stable armature or datum around which environmental change occurs? What is most desirable? Resilience? Diversity? Stability? Structural complexity? Openness to the unforeseen?

Rather than contributing to processes of retrieval or recuperation (restoration), might designers assume a more proactive stance by conceiving architectural interventions as (regimes of) *beneficial disturbance*? With such an outlook a designer would identify a gradient of possible disturbances, with level and type choreographed to site conditions, degree of degradation and simplification, and the purposes to which underutilized or sequestered resources might be put to work. Once an initial built disturbance has improved site conditions, designers are led to consider how the project might instigate, anticipate, and respond to those in the future.

As one approach to an urban architectural intervention as disturbance, a design team might, as part of a larger redevelopment strategy, adopt a "patch dynamics" non-equilibrium approach and create "gaps" within the impervious canopy of parking lots, roads and rooftops (similarly, a biogeography model might prompt the establishment of and connections between "islands" of open land in the urban tarmac).[18] Such gaps could fortify linkages between sun, sky, rain, plants, and soil, and elevate such interactions in human experience. New building projects accommodating gaps as morphological inspiration partake in an aesthetic of removal and informed, localized redistribution of matter. By engaging in processes of disruption, projects might establish habitat conservation areas (HCAs) in places not yet designated as such. They could serve as complexity-inducing entropies (stability-inducing disturbances), deterritorializations that reterritorialize: incisions, ruptures, scores, delaminations, splittings, and pryings apart. Gaps become "orderly frames for messy ecosystems," a notion championed by Joan Nassauer, prompting

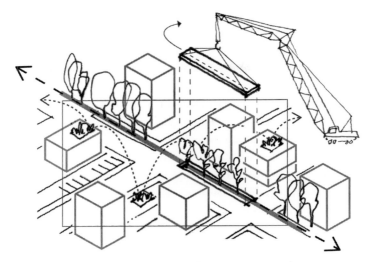

Design as strategic gap formation in the urban tarmac: connective green "stepping-stones" and corridors become integral components of project development.

processes that elevate locale-specific urban identity.[19] New projects fill in gaps strategically at the same time as new gaps form.

The transposition of a model for understanding the dynamics of forest ecosystems to processes of urban redevelopment is, at some level, fanciful speculation; blocks of buildings and stands of trees differ dramatically in structure, form, and behavior. And yet there is utility in reimagining the productive potential of the city; a project as a gap closes a gap and heals a wound.

A non-equilibrium model opens prospects for diversifying project goals by highlighting what it means to intervene in and alter systems processes unfolding over time. It fosters a tremendous sense of humility and responsibility, as design teams must acknowledge uncertainties and pay close attention to how projects affect trajectories of ecosystems in which they are situated. In embracing the open-endedness inherent to any consideration of what characterizes a well-functioning system, in coming to terms with the historical inseparability of human activity and the dynamics of natural systems, such a view invites the sorts of open "events" ecologies that political ecologists speak of while honoring the "intransigence" of the internal dynamics of ecosystem components.[20] The philosopher David Wood addresses this:

> If every living being does not merely have a relation to its outside, to what is other than itself, but is constantly managing that relationship economically (risking death for food, balancing individual advantage with collective prosperity, etc.), then however much it may be possible, for certain purposes, to treat such an environment collectively, that treatment will constantly be open to disruption from the intransigence of its parts.[21]

A non-equilibrium approach to an ecological architecture would accept the scaffold-like character of intentions and goals in a context of rapid environmental change and urbanization. As James Evans claims: "Non-equilibrium ... types of ecology are more sympathetic to the idiosyncrasies of urban nature."[22] Works of architecture as constructive mediums in ecological processes require long-term adaptive management strategies that entail, among other commitments, a willingness of communities to engage new disturbance regimes if original intentions differ from unforeseen eventualities.[23] Certain aspects of building assemblies will always be valued for their durability and stability. Others aspects can operate as more provisional purchases that give way as new needs and new ecologies form. One project may incorporate both the enduring and the provisional: the thermal/weather protective envelope for conditioned architectural space may be quite basic (box-like) as befits task and cost. Trellis-like, framed configurations may be deployed immediately adjacent to these envelopes as a means to condition them (to shade or otherwise modify light, to frame views, other) as well as to provide a platform for life to take root, climb, alight, and take flight.

Hierarchy model of ecosystems

Compelling contemporary theories of ecosystems acknowledge and attempt to reconcile divergent views, their value and influence lying in pluralistic conceptual

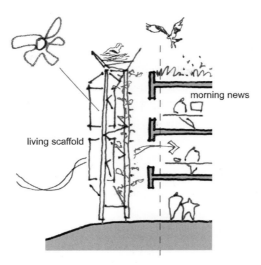

living scaffold

morning news

Scaffold-like armatures as extensions of both simple-skinned, light-filled buildings and ecologically rich surrounding (urban) environments.

synthesis. Proponents of **hierarchy theory**, for example, seek to align population/community and process/function understandings of ecosystems, two constructs often viewed as incompatible.[24] Hierarchy theorists maintain that the conclusions we draw about the characteristics of ecosystems depend largely on the spatiotemporal scale of observation. According to O'Neill *et al.*: "Depending on the observation set, ecosystems have been seen as static or dynamic, steady state or as fluctuating, as integrated systems or collections of individuals."[25] One set of conditions legitimizes an equilibrium model; with another observation set, a non-equilibrium view holds sway:

> Ecosystems can be viewed from many perspectives. Our conclusions are biased by the way we observe ecosystems. For example, if we focus on interactions among individual organisms, ecosystems seem relatively constant backgrounds, contexts in which interesting phenomena occur. If we focus on succession, ecosystems appear to change continuously through time. In fact, both impressions are correct, depending on the purpose and the time–space scale of our observations.[26]

Ecosystems are thus not discrete entities but models about systems derived from particular framings. This is a primary lesson for architects endeavoring to incorporate ecological concepts and theories in practice. As Haila and Levins argue: "In the end we are forced to recognize that the way we choose to identify the parts of a system depends very much on our purposes and tools."[27] Acknowledging this, one might even find and harmonize evidence of two seemingly competing tendencies operating simultaneously, for example, instances where function in an ecosystem is stable despite highly unstable populations. The summary caution, according to O'Neill *et al.*, is that "ecologists must be careful not to extrapolate from any single type of observation to the nature of the underlying system," and that "it is quite feasible and even reasonable to maintain an individualistic (i.e., Gleasonian) concept of community and a holistic concept of ecosystem function."[28]

Devised to assimilate multiple, "fragmentary realities," the hierarchy model organizes elements in ecosystems in levels corresponding to rates and frequencies. Lower-frequency components such as large stands of mature trees are a higher-level order, are less subject to perturbation (although subject nevertheless), and influence lower orders much more than the other way around (layers are asymmetrical in influence). Higher-frequency components such as microorganisms in the soil are lower in order, highly subject to perturbation, and influence higher orders much less than the other way around. Again, the hierarchy model offers a means of explaining dynamic conditions where sets of elements in ecosystems behave differently from others and where some have greater regulatory influence.

For the purposes of architectural design what may be of greatest significance in hierarchy theory is the idea that poorly connected systems can benefit and gain stability by the introduction of connecting elements. Conversely, strongly connected systems may break down suddenly in the face of disturbance. These systems may benefit from the introduction of constraining influences, for as O'Neill *et al.* suggest, an "ecosystem shows instability whenever the constraint system is broken down."[29] Given this view of weak versus strong connectivity, there may be value in asking, in reference to an urban site and neighborhood, what constraints have been removed and what sorts of stabilizing elements might be reintroduced. It may also be productive to consider how existing built elements that appear to function as physical constraints can act as biological enablers. For instance, a raised, bermed highway represents a significant barrier to movement for terrestrial species (and humans) occupying adjacent, low-lying lands. And yet Josh Cerra would encourage designers to think about reshaping and revegetating the highway right-of-way so as to divert movement (of snakes, for example) away from fast-moving traffic, to funnel species along routes parallel to the highway in order to reach underpasses and other through-connectors. A constraint in the urban context behaves as a "corridor of redirection," the very element that establishes a route of migration reduces risk and increases the long-term survival probabilities of city-dwelling species (note: hydrological and other barriers could also be deployed in this regard).[30]

Linking hierarchical structuring with the previous discussion of intermediate levels of disturbance in a non-equilibrium model, speculation as to whether interventions of "intermediate" scale frequency might have the greatest consequence in the performance of the system is warranted. A design investigation becomes a question of explicitly teasing out interactions of selected "in-between" layers and seeing how these can catalyze behaviors of components of higher and lower frequency. The "EcoDistrict," as opposed to the building or the city, becomes the focus, linking layers up and down the urban hierarchy. The EcoDistrict approach, as a filter of asymmetrical influences, informs the development of individual projects by situating them in context, assigning them roles as contributors to broader function, and promoting synergies and innovation between projects that may be unachievable in a demonstrative, timely, and politically feasible manner at a larger urban scale.

This brief, highly speculative consideration of a small number of ecological models suggests that multiple ecologies exist and points to the incompleteness of any one model, given the complexities to be reckoned with. For every model, even the non-equilibrium model that resonates in many ways with contemporary views of the world, certain conditions become obscured as others are highlighted. The notion of "buildings as disturbances," timely in capturing a contemporary tension and, as with any good metaphor, indicative of an ethical imperative, inspires designers to recalibrate assumptions about the purpose and meaning of projects they take on. Yet if the notion gains traction, the road does not lead to codification but instead prompts new questions and consideration of alternative models. Operating from an ethos of pluralism, rather than shifting from one pole to another, the interplay of multiple models assumes primacy. Designers are also encouraged to track syntheses of thought occurring with ecology itself, for example the development of the "neutral" theory that focuses on "drift" and that attempts a further reconciliation of the longstanding debate between equilibrium and non-equilibrium views.[31] By embracing these debates, architectural explorations may rebound to influence how ecologists think and work.

The linguist George Lakoff would consider ecology to be a "contested" metaphorical "source domain" in which semantic disturbance can operate as a productively creative force.[32] James Proctor and Brendon Hanson suggest: "By understanding metaphor as a necessary ally and not a threat to ecological knowledge, we may enrich our contextual understanding of (ecological) complexity while continuing to invoke it in useful ways."[33] James Corner builds on this argument:

> **It will be only through a more sophisticated understanding of ecology – one that transcends its status as a descriptive and analytical natural science and recognizes its metaphoricity as a cultural construction – that ecology's significance for a more creative and meaningful [landscape] architecture might be realized.[34]**

In furthering architectures inspired by hybrid conceptual constructs of natural processes and human activity, we should consider in greater detail the sway of deeply held metaphorical predispositions on architectural design thinking.

Notes

1   See Forsyth 2003.
2   Haila and Levins 1992, 73.

3 Taleb, 2007, xxvii.

4 Hubbell 2001, 8.

5 Kingsland 1991, 3.

6 Yeang 2006, 37, 24, and 31.

7 Might a mobile offer an appropriate metaphor for this view? The mobile moves gently as the summary of rotations of individual pieces. We touch it, prod it, redirect it, disrupt it and perhaps even damage it irrevocably.

8 O'Neill *et al.* 1986, 86.

9 Forsyth 2003, 68.

10 Alan Dickman, Director of the Environmental Studies Program at the University of Oregon, offers the following remarks on *disturbance*:

> "Contiguous concurrent mortality" was a definition suggested by my dissertation advisor, Stan Cook. It works as well as any other definition I've seen. One tree dying now and another in ten years isn't a disturbance. Many trees dying this year but at dispersed locations in the forest isn't necessarily a disturbance. But many trees dying in close proximity and the likely result of fire, or a logging operation, or a windstorm or landslide: that is a disturbance.
>
> (Personal correspondence, November 2011)

11 See for example Dempster 2007.

12 Pickett and White 1985, 383.

13 Pickett and White 1985, 8–9.

14 Personal correspondence with Fred Swanson, May 2010.

15 Norton 1987, 52.

16 See for example Pulliam and Johnson 2002, 223–224.

17 Holling 1973, 15.

18 See Pickett and White 1985.

19 See Nassauer 1995.

20 For a discussion of events ecology, see Forsyth 2003.

21 Wood 2005, 162.

22 Evans 2007, 146.

23 For a treatment of adaptive management strategies, see Norton 2005.

24 This discussion of hierarchy theory builds from O'Neill *et al.* 1986.

25   O'Neill *et al.* 1986, 20.

26   O'Neill *et al.* 1986, 3.

27   Haila and Levins 1992, 47.

28   O'Neill *et al.* 1986, 19 and 189.

29   O'Neill *et al.* 1986, 211.

30   Personal correspondence with Peg Boulay, Co-Director of the
     Environmental Leadership Program in the Environmental Studies Program
     at the University of Oregon, October 14, 2012.

31   See Hubbell 2001.

32   See Lakoff 2006.

33   Proctor and Larson 2005, 166.

34   Corner 1997, x.

Part II

Conceptual (Eco)architectural Constructs

CHAPTER 4

Metaphor and Respatialization

Metaphor is not suspended from natural reality, but that in opening up meaning on the imaginative side it also opens it up toward a dimension of reality that does not coincide with what ordinary language envisages under the name of natural reality.[1]

Just as texts are built, so buildings are written.[2]

Architects tend to view metaphors as peripheral to the design process. The end game of finished works of architecture, edifices that stand against wind and rain, encourages de-emphasis on indirect and less tangible forms of communication. The architect turned away from an unsatisfying postmodern affair with literary theory and committed to essential matters: green cities, new urbanisms, phenomenology, intelligent skins, prefabrication, and information modeling. In their anthology on sustainable architectures, Simon Guy and Steven Moore capture a prevailing view by suggesting: "While we might support and even encourage critical engagement with abstract theory about environmentalism, we are not interested in simply playing language games."[3]

Because architects rely on metaphors to describe and execute design intentions, they inevitably play games of great consequence: games for gathering, symbolizing, disarming, and outrunning the competition. In preliminary phases of architectural design, the merit of a conceptual organizational idea corresponds to its capacity to make arresting aspects of the project deemed critically important while anticipating a host of other concerns eventually requiring careful assimilation (whether or not they are highlighted initially). Building scientist G.Z. Brown explains:

> Building design is a creative process based on iteration: one begins by
> responding to a situation with an abstract idea. Then one objectifies the idea,

by proposing a trial design, evaluates it, redesigns it, develops it, reevaluates it, and so on.[4]

Striving for coherence and memorability given a density of conditions and requirements – legal, practical, political, aesthetic, economic, environmental, topographic – is paramount to design success. Metaphors can assist in synthesizing this complex array.

Metaphor's succinct, combinatory density creates a charged atmosphere that helps form community. Ted Cohen's considerations of this aspect of metaphor are worth quoting at some length:

> I want to suggest a point in metaphor which is independent of the question of its cognivity and which has nothing to do with its aesthetical character. I think of this point as the achievement of intimacy. There is a way in which the maker and the appreciator of metaphor are drawn closer to one another. Three aspects are involved: (1) The speaker issues a kind of concealed invitation; (2) The hearer extends a special effort to accept the invitation; and (3) this transaction constitutes the acknowledgement of a community. All three are involved in any communication, but in ordinary literal discourse their involvement is so pervasive and routine that they go unremarked. The use of metaphor throws them into relief, and there is a point in that.[5]

Booth complements Cohen in offering criteria that help determine a metaphor's success: it should be active, concise, appropriate, accommodating of the audience, and building of a proper ethos.[6] All of these qualities are pertinent to the ability to practice effectively in the complex social realm in which architecture unfolds; a metaphor might help establish a sought-after, shared, ethical, and aesthetically malleable awareness within the project team and between the team and clients and the larger community with and for whom they work. (Contrary to Cohen's claim, aesthetic sensibility would seem a valuable trait in offering an invitation that is attractive.)

Evocative, project-specific metaphors may assist in the creation of a shared vision as the design team travels along an iterative path of architectural innovation over an extended period of time. David Cook, partner in the Stuttgart-based practice Haas Cook Zemmrich, suggests: "Metaphors are particularly important on large projects where we need to have shared long-term goals and where the architecture may be something which is to a large extent still in flux."[7] Cook also notes that

> **The quality of the realized building is more often than not dependent upon the strength of the original idea, [and while] I think most metaphors tend to be a little diffuse at the commencement of a project, they then become more defined as the project progresses.**[8]

Drawings and words shape each other over time.

Designers employ metaphors frequently and out of communicative necessity while denying their significance with a kind of oversight that hinders ability to operate more self-critically. In their study on metaphor in the architectural design process, Coyne *et al*. argue: "The greatest privileging occurs when certain metaphors are so taken for granted that they are not generally seen as metaphors."[9] Similarly, Iris Marion Young brings awareness to the ideological function of metaphors "when they represent the context in which they arise as natural or necessary."[10] Even as simple a notion as "architects design buildings," one that appears distinctly and transparently non-metaphorical, reveals a strong metaphorical impetus, prioritizing but one dimension, albeit a highly significant one, of the architectural enterprise. In the sense that one could consider an act of architecture as furnishing an urban room (fitting out the interstices and gaps of the city), demarcating the landscape, positioning interior spaces within a complex ensemble, choreographing the work of teams involved in design and construction, or expressing societal commitment to equitable access to the dignity of shelter, "making buildings" serves as a concise, memorable metaphorical stand-in for – and to a certain extent displacement of – a more encompassing set of acts and meanings.

This is not to say "building" is a poor metaphor for architecture – so often this conceptual orientation leads to such beautiful outcomes (!) – only that the notion of architecture-as-building weds problem and solution too quickly. Operating as a boundary domain, the metaphor foregrounds and settles the challenge of architecture as a certain kind of arrangement (of built components) with a certain bandwidth of expression (projection of arrangement in negotiation with others of a kind). Given the urgency of environmental problems, we should slow down for a moment and consider its hold on the imaginary.

Linguist George Lakoff and philosopher Mark Johnson demonstrate powerfully how metaphors are more than simply imaginative flourishes and instead shape processes of thought and descriptions of reality, offering a "systematicity that allows us to comprehend one aspect of a concept in terms of another."[11] They describe in detail relationships between a metaphor's "source domain" (the domain borrowed from to describe something) and its "target domain" (the domain demanding explanation). Critically, not all attributes associated with the source domain transfer to its target, especially those that are immediately obvious. Lakoff and Johnson describe the characteristics that do transfer as constituting a *coherent network of entailments* that illuminate certain possibilities while concealing others.

More than a clever substituting of terms, metaphors compress the pattern of migration of a system. The metaphorical notion *"architecture is the making of buildings"* involves transferring certain qualities from "building" as source domain to "architecture" as target domain that may include the following entailments:

- Architecture consists in the making of tangible, material entities.
- Such entities are discrete (freestanding, object-like).
- Individual elements (bricks, windows, walls) are configured in such a way as to emphasize a building's completeness; architectural aesthetics focuses on expression, arrangement and resolution of discrete elements within a clearly defined field (site, area or volume).
- Buildings are the building blocks of larger entities – blocks, neighborhoods, cities – also to be understood as discrete.

Downplayed in this view of an architectural intervention are systems that nest within and link to larger systems in the outside world (energy, water, and communications systems, to name a few). Also deemphasized are the ways projects act on and are shaped in turn by climatic and other environmental forces. The architect integrates these systems and takes stock of these forces, they are part of a building's fabric and are necessary for its inhabitability, yet she/he may not privilege these as deserving expressive and perceptual register. They exist but are not what matters.

Varela *et al.* view metaphors as a means to accommodate complexities in a manner influencing the kinds of research questions, and therefore the kinds of new knowledge, that might be generated and considered legitimate within the domain of cognitive science.[12] Characterizations of knowledge creation in sustainable architectural design, metaphorical carryovers from the movement's predecessors, "naturally" emphasize buildings, parts of buildings, and acts of building. As with other disciplines and domains of inquiry, prominent are notions such as creating a foundation and adding to it, laying an intellectual groundwork, constructing an argument, erecting pillars and edifices, establishing frames of reference and frameworks of understanding, providing a window to shed light on certain conditions, meeting critical thresholds, and ensuring adequate underpinnings. Architects utilize "toolkits" of design strategies in order to achieve greater efficiencies in the application of knowledge, for example in efforts to save energy or to streamline project coordination. In setting up milestones, critical paths, conceptual bridges, and landmarks of innovative thought, architects, like others, describe dimensions of knowledge as demarcation and regularization of the landscape.

These conventions presume a stable context that new knowledge "builds upon": designers can apply well-honed tools that adjust to and match up optimally with relatively finite questions of design, and in so doing can help erect an edifice that further discloses the dynamic forms of reality. Missing from ways of describing architectural knowledge is acknowledgment of "outlier" events common to design investigation that stimulate the process by providing the impetus to rework conceptual categories. In addition, these ways of speaking about buildings, knowledge, and "knowledge building" fail to account for new forms of ignorance that new understandings generate. According to the sociologist Matthias Gross: "The contemporary explosion of knowledge or the observation that our current age is the beginning of a knowledge society thus has a little remarked on corollary: new knowledge also means more ignorance."[13]

Designers are poorly equipped to discuss the role of knowledge in a time of rapid ecological degradation, where the environment can no longer be viewed as a neutral backdrop to human affairs. Enhanced ecological literacy pertains not only to nature's rules but additionally to how levels of complexity exceeding the most dependable indicators and rule-governed modeling tools alter what is meant by soundness in the assimilation of knowledge. Renewing commitments amidst the proliferation of non-knowledge encourages expanding frames of reference, deploying multiple frames as a means to register other kinds of difference, and owning up to the limitations of any composite.[14]

The language of sustainable architecture, emphasizing the building proper and a small envelope around it, can seem impoverished relative to a diverse range of environmental conditions it might account for. In her consideration of ways architects discuss air, philosopher Helen Mallinson finds excessive reliance on terms such as "R-value," "Btu," "infiltration," "vapor barrier," "air changes per hour" and the like. For her this limited vocabulary has grave consequences:

> The outstanding problem for architectural theory ... is that it seems at a loss for words when it comes to the air. How then, one might ask, can it contribute to any serious discussion on the ethics of sustaining the earth's most extraordinary architectural shelter, the atmosphere?[15]

In a profession so reliant on effective communication, in an era when imperatives of sustainability motivate inquiry, designers should not underestimate the ways originative narratives of expression influence the atmosphere in which architectural investigations occur. Architecture as more outwardly dynamic, poetic, and graceful receptivity towards the environment can be instantiated by what the environmental philosopher Bryan Norton considers "linguistic activism."[16]

Given high levels of predictability and standardization in architecture in contemporary society, metaphors help create space for the acknowledgment of the particularity of a situation, or that which fails to receive the attention it deserves in everyday affairs. The value and necessity of metaphorical novelty become apparent when the designer confronts unusual situations and strives to share unfamiliar ideas with stakeholders. A metaphor may suggest itself to a design team member in the conceptual design phase, revealing for all enriched discernment as to the specific nature of the problem and perhaps larger aspirations for what architecture can be. Timely metaphors can help designers displace old meanings, open and expand a system of relations, generate new patterns of enunciation, and bridge ideas formerly unrelated.

Patterns of articulation and habits of behavior inscribe themselves upon one another; unmarked in the daily bustle are ways, as environmental writer Michael D. Cohen evocatively puts it, "present systems are landmarks of earlier contest."[17] Patterns calcify over time, and may become dissonant relative to the dynamically evolving conditions a design culture is called upon to respond to. An ushering in of new possibilities at critical times registers with cultural anthropologist Clifford Geertz' conviction of *incongruity* as a vital dimension of metaphor and art historian Henri Focillon's assertion that "there is no meaning without displacement of meaning, without metaphor."[18]

Linguist George Steiner speaks to the creative striving necessary to find short-lived equilibrium in a linguistic environment subject to recurring disturbance: "Fundamental energies of adjustment between language and human need lie precisely in the logically recalcitrant zone."[19] Steiner further argues:

> But it is the great untidiness that makes human speech innovative and expressive of personal intent. It is the anomaly, as it feeds back into the general history of usage, as it enriches and complicates the general standard of definition, which gives coherence to the system. A coherence, if such a description is allowed, in constant motion.[20]

Deriving meaning involves grouping entities with common or similar attributes into assemblages, and displacing and singularizing based on these categorizations (family, genus, species, individual). Recognition of a particular involves its emergence from a background field of categorization. Unkempt and playfully novel juxtapositions exert force upon habits of practice, foster recognition of new particulars, and set the familiar against a different relief. Metaphors that associate larger-scale natural systems, habitat structures, and singular architectural propositions may prove especially rewarding and resourceful in their nuance. Permeability of thought, awareness of a range of conceptual possibilities embedded within a chosen vocabulary, parallels the specifying of permeable pavers in construing design elements in richly associative and functionally expressive ways. The eventual assimilation of the particular, the dissolution of anomaly, reworks the dimensions of the categorical playing field.

Metaphors as acts of respatialization

That metaphors gain coherence through systematic transfer of properties (entailments) helps explain why so many are spatial or otherwise tangible in origin. As Lakoff and Johnson demonstrate: "We typically conceptualize the non physical in terms of the physical – that is, we conceptualize the less clearly delineated in terms of the more clearly delineated."[21] Events and entities that register to the senses, that comprise our embodied experience, enable intricate modeling of complex possibility. To grasp furnishes such an example: an idea is something we hold in the palm of our hand; we turn it around, feel it, and study it from many angles in order to appreciate its numerous facets.

While Lakoff and Johnson contend that "most of our fundamental concepts are organized in terms of one or more spatialization metaphors," the architect working with metaphors performs an act of *respatialization*.[22] A tangible, experience-based spatial understanding provides a more abstract metaphorical conception that in turn offers an impetus for architectural space-making. Louis Kahn's famous dictum for the Phillips Exeter Library in New Hampshire, "taking a book and bringing it to the light," provides a wonderfully elaborated example of this process. A conceptual notion (how we gain knowledge) originates in embodied experience (vision made possible by the presence of light, such that light-enabling vision = knowledge). Kahn projects this construct back upon the

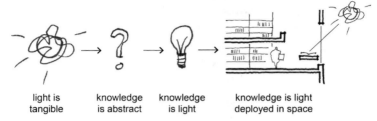

light is | knowledge | knowledge | knowledge is light
tangible | is abstract | is light | deployed in space

Louis Kahn's inspirational notion of "taking a book and bringing it to the light" for the design of the Exeter Public Library is an example of the architect performing an act of "respatialization."

physical realm through patterns of spatio-luminous organization "embodied" in the library: one literally takes a book from a low-ceilinged and relatively dark stack space and brings it to a generously daylit study carrel at the building's periphery.

This famously compelling example illustrates how metaphorical respatialization as one dimension of the design process can encourage charged simultaneity of the cerebral, kinetic, studied, and sensed; impression and act, knowledge, contemplative view, passage, and immersion in a book exceed and speak volumes. It encapsulates a dense set of acts and begins to touch on the straightforward yet rigorously elaborated architectural ensemble necessary to support them. In the context of ecological uncertainty, of concern in subsequent chapters are how metaphors as respatializations begin to suggest the manner in which architectural interventions interact with a surrounding set of spaces and conditions, as opposed to highlighting organizations of a purer resolution. Of particular interest are metaphors that encourage successive alternations in scale of emphasis, recenter the target domain, and in so doing call into question the indisputability of the source and suggest projects as activators of systems (whether the activation pertains to concentration, diversion, or cycling) and that are acted upon in turn. Also desirable are those metaphors encouraging extension to other domains of disciplinary inquiry. Proctor and Larson's view of metaphors as "nomadic terms linking disciplines" seems especially useful as the ecological respatialization of architecture proceeds outward.[23]

Notes

1　Ricoeur 1977, 211.
2　Casey 1997, 310.
3　Guy and Moore 2005, 2.
4　Brown 1990, 2.
5　Cohen 1978, 1–2.
6　See Booth 1978.
7　Personal correspondence with David Cook, July 18, 2007.
8　Personal correspondence with David Cook, July 18, 2007.
9　Coyne *et al.* 1994, 114.
10　Young 1990, 74.
11　Lakoff and Johnson 1980, 10.
12　See Varela *et al.* 1991.
13　Gross 2010, 1.
14　The architectural community does a better job engaging uncertainty and paradox than it does talking about these matters. One primary reason is that a client investing handsomely in new building or renovation and who seeks a stable investment is not interested in an architect's professions of ignorance.
15　Mallinson 2004, 177.
16　See Norton 2005.
17　Cohen 1998, 9.
18　Geertz 1973, 210; Focillon 1992, 26.
19　Steiner 1998, 226.
20　Steiner 1998, 213.
21　Lakoff and Johnson 1980, 59.
22　Lakoff and Johnson 1980, 17. As psychologist Barbara Tversky describes it: "When thought overwhelms the mind, the mind puts thoughts into the world" (from "Tools of Thought," lecture delivered at the University of Oregon in May 2013).
23　Proctor and Larson 2005, 1066.

CHAPTER 5

Bodies

The shape of a metaphor and the system of entailments that provide its structure adjust to atmospheric pressures of cultural change. A light tracing of a history of metaphors emphasizing embodied and organism-like dimensions of architecture speaks to their persistence and evolution. Ideas of bodies and beings linger in the present and, in association with related metaphorical constructs, weigh on questions of the depth and form of an ecological architecture.

The flesh and bone of the concept of the body are mediated and understood intellectually, culturally, and theologically. "Body" operates as a node within a network of other entities: landscapes, nature(s), god(s), other bodies (human and nonhuman), inorganic elements, etc. Evolving views of architectural embodiment correlate to a repositioning of the body's status within this open

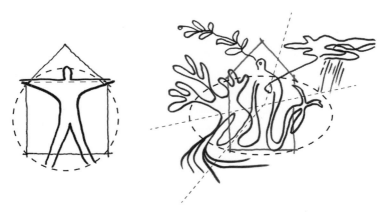

Architecture will always be bodies and for bodies, the specific manifestations of which will depend on a changing set of conceptual relations (between bodies and buildings, buildings and the landscape, etc.).

system of relations. The notion of *architecture as body* necessarily implies a larger conceptual sensibility and poetic worldview that encompasses humans, humanity, animality, the global, and the divine.

Qualities of surface, form, proportion, and harmony inform the body of architecture during the Renaissance. The shapeliness of the human body, the closest earthly facsimile to God's ordered perfection, provides an ideal from which to design building façades and other elements of architectural composition. The Neoplatonist Renaissance philosopher Marsilio Ficino considers the uniqueness of human beings a function of their role as privileged intermediaries binding the plurality of the worldly (nature) to heavenly oneness (the apex of God). Ficino envisions a *pyramidal* structure, establishing, as Alberto Perez-Gomez describes, "a hierarchy of being that emanates from God (unity) and extends down to the physical world (multiplicity)."[1] Works of architecture as embodiments of humankind lift worldly mortality toward God's perfection, for, as Perez-Gomez articulates: "Through them the splendour of beauty contributes to reconcile multiplicity into unity."[2]

Significantly, and something overlooked in Perez-Gomez's writings, Ficino's pyramidal hierarchy relies on an understanding of the discreteness of species. As the scholar of Renaissance humanism Paul Kristeller contends, in discussing this system: "The whole sphere of being ... is constructed out of substantial entities that coexist in a definite order."[3] For Ficino:

> The importance of species rests essentially upon the fact that each species is distinguished from the others through its ranking, but does not admit further graded differences within itself, in other words, between its individual members.[4]

Ultimately, Kristeller concludes: "The single species, therefore, constitutes the different degrees of being, and the whole universe, as a unique hierarchy, is constructed upon the different species."[5] Only through the singularity of species derived from the sameness of kind can one comprehend an overarching unity.[6] Although stationed above the multiple, man, like other beings of divine creation, has a stable and fixed corporeal identity. Individual works of architecture as singular acts of aesthetic and technical rigor affirm and figure in – as in helping to discern a figure – a system of immutable forms.

As high artistic pursuit, architectural design is the seeking of truth of the structure of nature. Works of architecture validate a metanarrative patterned on firmness of place of living beings. A spatial metaphor encompassing life and afterlife ennobles architectural creation. In considering the philosophical orientation of the seventeenth-century statesman the Earl of Shaftesbury, British literary theorist Terry Eagleton discusses this metaphysical and metacultural striving:

> **Truth for this passed over Platonist is an artistic apprehension of the world's inner design: to understand something is to grasp its proportioned place in the whole, and is so at once cognitive and aesthetic. Knowledge is a creative intuition which discloses the dynamic forms of nature.[7]**

The species as building block continues to structure descriptions of natural order in a dominant strain of intellectual history that follows. A system of classification confronts the multitudinous chaos of life. Species as types with transcendental geometric figures define positions within complex taxonomies. Enlightened rationalist architectural theorists emphasize the correspondence of building to type as the key to architectural meaning. The human body again serves as privileged geometrical model.

The shape of contemporary discourse pertaining to architectures of bodies, organisms, and environments is still influenced by Enlightenment ideas of types and taxonomy, as it is by the organic romanticism of the late eighteenth century (oneness of all of life and matter achieving manifest perfection in human creativity) and the revolutionary explosiveness of the Darwinian evolutionary economy. It is likewise shaped by an inward turn of understanding of (human) beings at the beginning of the twentieth century, past surface and through form, in an interchange of meaning and innovation among disciplines such as biology, philosophy, and psychology. In Vienna, insight into the depths of inner conflict influences architectural thinking, as does the idea that outward appearances are less than pure projections of – and in ways concealments of – darker forces within. Freud's illuminations on the unconscious parallel Viennese Secessionist architects' interest in the design of façades for multi-story urban buildings as cloak-like skins intimating mysteriously complex interiors, the preserves of domestic arrangements (that are in turn inhibiting shelters of personal drive). The Slovenian-born architect Josef Plecnik's Zacherl House (1904–1905) furnishes an example of this approach. The articulation of polished gray granite plates that make up the façade intimate the structure of an inner order without divulging it; the curving corner adds to the appearance of figural tailoring.

In the 1920s and the decades that follow, advancements in understanding the genetics of organisms decenters language of the body such that the human figure no longer occupies a privileged location. Notions of replication, coded transmission, internal realignments, and a "highly coordinated system of regulatory dynamics" characterize descriptions of an organism's formation and

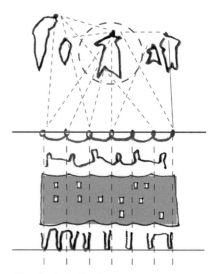

Viennese "surface effects": cloak-like skins intimating complex interiors.

development.[8] Fox Keller relates the "information exchange" view of organisms to the conceptual exchanges occurring between developmental biology and the more established domain of molecular biology: "It was the metaphorical use of information as it criss-crossed among these two sets of disciplines, their practitioners, and among their subjects – that provided the principal vector for the dissemination of meaning."[9]

At mid-century, "vectors" of linguistic transmission fortify; with the emergence of cybernetics and a growing emphasis on a systems view of flows of information within bodies and beyond, organisms and machines become conflated increasingly:

> **Can it be any surprise, then, that in the bootstrap process of modeling organisms and machines, each upon the other, not only do organisms and machines come increasingly to resemble one another but, as they do, the meaning of both terms undergoes some rather critical changes?[10]**

Electro-mechanistic dispositions pervade discourse on the bodies of living beings in the natural sciences. In evolutionary developmental biology, a scientific arena of expansive cultural impact, assemblages of switches and currents determine bodily formation such that, as Sean Carroll maintains: "Animal *architecture* is a product of genetic regulatory network."[11] Carroll further articulates:

> **The key to innovation at the genetic level is the multifunctionality of tool kit genes. The multifunctionality of tool kit genes stems from their deployment at different times and places through batteries of genetic switches.[12]**

Contemporary design culture embraces this esteemed language of animal architecture. Routed through systems thinking and cybernetics, bio/eco terms such as adaptability, resilience, cellular, generative, emergent, and symbiotic influence architectural design explorations, in particular those driven digitally. Small-scale biological phenomena such as genetic "switches," the channeling and selective inhibition of information flows, and other processes determining the growth of the organism inspire a new design generation interested in

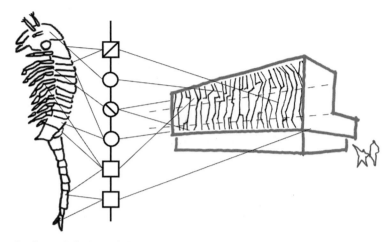

Smaller-scale biological phenomena (organisms) influencing the design of buildings and parts of buildings.

rule-governed architectural morphology. A body is once again projected upon a building's surface but it is a different body requiring higher levels of magnification.

While there is much to be said for conceptualizing buildings as organisms, this manner of thought has tended to produce relatively limited, insular experiments focusing on scaling up smaller biological phenomena in order to design individual works of architecture or significant components of them. In this body-to-building mapping, architects borrow biological and ecological terms in ways that may not significantly impact the trajectory of development relative to the ecology of the city. Even highly progressive "green" conceptual constructs in architecture today can lead to a perpetuation of emphasis on the carapace-like skin of a building proper and thin layers of ambient and luminous tension surrounding it. In "Ecological Aesthetics in Architecture: A Deadwood Metaphor," Leonard Yui scrutinizes this ostensibly beneficial standard of "living buildings," suggesting that it might encourage a one-way movement where the designer appropriates particular entailments carried in the metaphor (organisms such as flowers with petals) in order to "animate" architecture.[13]

While providing a powerful framework to develop building systems that achieve aggressive levels of performance, and while encouraging sharing of resources and development of solutions that extend beyond a project area, the basic metaphorical characterization of a goal of realizing a living building may be more iconic than relational, and therefore limiting.

With conscious irony, Yui counters "living buildings" with the notion of "dead buildings" as in "deadwood." Harkening to processes that facilitate energy and material flows and that establish well-functioning forest ecosystems, architectural assemblies as "snags," "fallen logs," and nutritive purchases may be better suited to the creation of diverse living communities than those conceptualized as alive. "Deadwood" as primary descriptor encourages the view of architectures as participants in more encompassing acts of regeneration. Site-scale design interventions operate as catalysts within broader-scale ecological systems by serving as stepping-stones for nonhuman species to reach fragmented habitat patches, aggressively treating stormwater so as to support watershed health, and acting as "beneficial disturbances" that help elevate the function of biologically compromised urban sites. Interestingly, although the deadwood metaphor focuses on the building/built entity, it prompts a manner of thinking as far as the interface of building skin and form and dynamics of the surrounding landscape.

Works of architecture as nutrient-rich purchases akin to fallen logs in a forest ecosystem (inspired by Yui 2010).

With an outlook sympathetic to Yui's, and with an eye on alternatives to previously discussed construal of organisms as encasements of genetic phenomena, evolutionary biologist and social commentator Richard Lewontin argues: "The metaphor of computation is just a trendy form of Descartes' metaphor of the machine."[14] Eschewing narrow, mechanistic description, Lewontin emphasizes co-conditionings of organism and environment: an organism has inward structural disposition at the same time it assumes, through "triggered" cues from its *Umwelt*, a selective set of rhythmic links to the outerworld. (*Umwelt* corresponds to Richard Dawkins' notion of an "extended phenotype" and refers to an organism's "model" of its environment, meaning its "self-centering" within its surrounding world, its manner of negotiating it, making sense of it, modifying it, and surviving within it. Two organisms can occupy the same environment yet live within different *Umwelten*.)

Mark Johnson maintains:

> **As Levins and Lewontin have argued, natural selection is not a consequence of how well the organism solves a set of problems posed by the environment;**

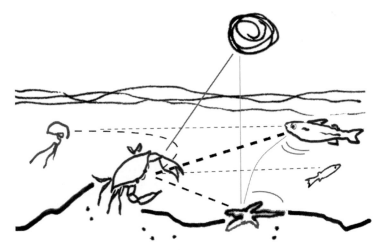

> Organisms engage in a melodic set of exchanges with one another and with inorganic elements in their surroundings.

on the contrary, the environment and the organism actively codetermine each other. The internal and external factors, genes and the environment, act upon each other through the medium of the organism.[15]

A major dimension to the phenomenologist Maurice Merleau-Ponty's philosophical project involved a reconstitution of the body through an intertwining of body and *Umwelt*. He drew heavily from the German biologist Jacob von Uexküll to explicate this view, as did other philosophers such as Giorgio Agamben who were attracted to this conception:

> Everything happens as if the external carrier of significance (marks in the *Umwelt* or environment-world perceived by the organism) and its receiver in the animal's body constituted two elements in a single musical score.[16]

This actively relational orientation, focused less exclusively on internal biological circuitry and more on melodic exchange at the porous boundaries of beings and environments, influences certain contemporary readings of architecture. According to Marie-Ange Brayer:

> The frame, the frontier, the wall, the barrier – all giving way to the passage, the membrane, the network and all the other mediators between the body and its environment, between architecture and the dynamic processes that structure it.[17]

Behnisch and Partners' IBN (Dutch) Institute for Forestry Nature and Research in Wageningen, the Netherlands, provides an example of ecologically minded architecture as an embodiment of dynamic interaction between a project and its milieu. In 1993, the Stuttgart-based firm won a competition for their design for the IBN, a European Union pilot project for "human and environmentally-friendly building."[18] During the competition phase and throughout the life of the project, the design team elaborated in narrative and graphic form architectural qualities corresponding to those of a complex organism. Architecture as a dynamically interactive organism operated in concert with other conceptual drivers in informing design thinking with respect to the project in its entirety, to fine detail, and most critically to how its parts related to the IBN's setting, a mixture of agricultural and suburban lands within the Rhine watershed in the eastern part of the Netherlands.

A formation of 60 × 100 foot "postage stamp"-shaped gardens arranged axially serve as the project's primary organizational structure. Each garden represents a regional biotope; a grassland garden, a marsh garden, a woodland garden, etc. Each of three office wings is situated between two of the gardens and is said to "**grow** between the gardens." As formative gesture, the garden structure provides stability for the building-as-organism to find "purchase," offering a niche that is both flexible and distinct.

The IBN as *organism* coheres within itself. Its internal organizational logic is the residue of past articulations: the inclinations and previous experiences of the designer, the programmatic needs of the client, the technical rigors of building as embodied in the "code," etc. At the same time, the IBN "contains a reference to its future."[19] In the likely event that the institute's scope and mission evolve, that it secures grants, hires researchers, and finds itself in need of additional space, the garden structure and laboratory **wing** to the north anticipate the location of new construction. The adaptable portions of the

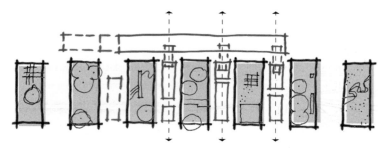

"The building grows between the gardens": building elements gain purchase within a coherent landscape structure (concept diagram for Behnisch and Partners Architects' Dutch Institute for Forestry Nature and Research, Wageningen, the Netherlands, 1993–1996).

building unfurl against a fixed armature (garden). Merleau-Ponty's notion of organism as described by Mark Hansen is illuminating of both inhabitation and inhabitant-initiated architectural response: "Behavior is what transforms such intrinsic potentiality into history while simultaneously preserving it as a 'source' for future growth."[20] The IBN is incomplete, is never complete but "weak formed," existing in a perpetual state of tense fitness, ever adaptable to changing needs and the disquiet of persistent animation within.

Single-glazed greenhouses, inexpensive and off-the-shelf, span gardens between office wings. The atria thus created serve as the offices' **"lungs,"** capturing and retaining warmth in winter, enabling dramatic downsizing of the heating system, and channeling cooling breezes in summer, obviating the need for air conditioning. Because the greenhouse roofs provide a first layer of protection against the elements, the office façades are single-glazed, "porous" centers of sensation, **skins** that actively, selectively absorb and transmit (the wanted) and refract and transform (the unwanted). With offices facing and open to gardens, the atria become the institute's social **heart**, where scientists gather, conduct research, and confer.

The IBN holds true to a contemporary understanding, as described by Robert Mugerauer, of both "the unity of the organism, and the dynamic, interactive

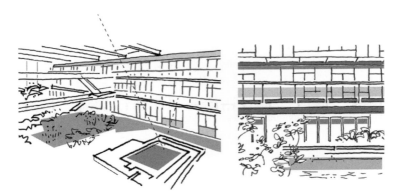

Views of atrium space in the Dutch Institute for Forestry and Nature Research.

relationship that organisms have with their environments."[21] A play exists between the IBN's intrinsic dispositions and those entities and phenomena with which it is engaged in the *Umwelt* to which it adheres. Again Merleau-Ponty on the organism: "We have a section (intersection) that creates a new territory, and the place of the section decides what will be regenerated because it prescribes to the internal dynamic what it has to produce in order to retrieve its equilibrium."[22] There is a thematic open-endedness to the adjustment of vent openings and deployment of operable shades in the IBN's greenhouse roofs and porous façades and the drawing of cool air across the concrete mass (corpus) of office floors, a setting into action prescribed by the disequilibrium created by changes in surroundings – shifts in temperature, light, and movement of air. As with many projects, an abstracted body provides the figural impetus for a functionally resourceful organizational strategy, one of localized symmetries in acknowledgment of a non-neutral, asymmetrically charged enveloping milieu.

Behnisch and Partners' metaphorical appropriation of attributes of an organism may be regarded as a vehicle for aestheticization. Yet a favorable view of aestheticization may be set forth, a "relational" one in Bourriad's sense,[23] implicated in our actions and artifacts and in agreement with Dewey's assertion that "esthetic effect is due to art's unique transcript of the energy of things of the world."[24] Inseparability of appearance and behavior, expression and content, distinguishes the IBN and works like it. As but one example, greenhouses and "extensive" moss sedum office roofs collect rainwater diverted to reflecting pools in atria gardens, where it is available for irrigation of garden plantings. Evapotranspiration by the plants helps cool the atria and adjacent offices. Bench-like platforms built into the sides of reflecting pools provide a contemplative setting for IBN staff to take work breaks. In this instance and throughout the project, ambiguity exists as to where aesthetic concerns trail off and where functional, ecological, spatial, or thermodynamic conditions begin. Merleau-Ponty suggests that "animals' acts are the manifestation of a certain style" and "instinct is before all else a theme, a style that meets up with that which evokes it in its milieu."[25] As with the animal, the IBN's patterning of functioning behavior is style inseparable from action.

Despite the emphasis in the preceding discussion, critically important is the fact that the IBN project team entertained multiple metaphors, *project as garden* and *project as city* as examples, in addition to organism. Rich architectures – the effectiveness of translation from conception to drawing to building – require the free commerce of plural images: buildings as organisms and landscapes, bodies within gardens of buildings, cities as systems of ecologies.[26] Seams of scalar and combinatory thinking encourage creation of diverse spatio-thermal gradients generated from highly economical material assemblages. Entailments derived from several source domains cast simple sets of architectural features in complex parts.

Notes

1 Perez-Gomez 2006, 75.
2 Perez-Gomez 2006, 75.
3 Kristeller 1943, 74.
4 Kristeller 1943, 81.
5 Kristeller 1943, 82.
6 Notably, centuries later, anthropologist and ethnologist Lévi-Strauss would look to species diversity as a basis for a fragmented versus a unified whole: "The diversity of species furnishes man with the most intuitive picture at his disposal and constitutes the most direct manifestation he can produce of the ultimate discontinuity of reality" (see Lévi-Strauss 1966, 137).
7 Eagleton 1990, 35.
8 Fox Keller 1995, 30.
9 Fox Keller 1995, 104.
10 Fox Keller 1995, 108.
11 Carroll 2005, 129 (italics added).
12 Carroll 2005, 288.
13 See Yui 2010; for information on living buildings see: http://living-future. org.
14 Lewontin 2000, 38.
15 Johnson 1987, 2007.
16 Agamben 2004, 41.

17 Brayer 2003, 18.

18 The description is a first-hand account as I worked for Behnisch and Partners from 1993 to 1997 and was a lead member of the IBN design team from the competition phase through construction.

19 Hansen 2005, 239.

20 Hansen 2005, 239.

21 Mugerauer 2004, 193.

22 Merleau-Ponty 2003, 234.

23 See Bourriaud 2002.

24 Dewey 1980, 185.

25 Merleau-Ponty 2003, 192 and 193.

26 "Translations from drawing to building" is a reference to Evans 1997.

CHAPTER 6

Furnishings

People who have not lost the wholeness of their place can see their households and their regional mountains or woods as within the same sphere.[1]

Lightness goes for me with precision and determination, and not with vagueness and the haphazard.[2]

furnish, v.t. 1. to provide or supply, often fol. by with: to furnish one with needed time. 2. to fit out, a house, room, etc., with necessary appliances, esp. furniture.[3]

In a two-week design charrette, the instructor team for the 2001 Glenn Murcutt Architecture Master Class asked student teams to design a gallery in a bowl-shaped meadow adjacent to the Arthur and Yvonne Boyd Art Centre at Riversdale, West Cambewarra, a rural area of eucalypt-clad hills in New South Wales.[4] During an early morning site visit, instructor and architect Richard Leplastrier appealed to design students to consider their role as "furnishing with particular purpose this larger room we are in." This strikingly succinct, deceptively complex metaphorical notion redirected subsequent inquiry from design of a building proper to more focused attention on spatial, thermal, luminous, and other attributes of the landscape. Recognition that a room exists and provides some measure of comfort challenged design teams to extend their thinking, question levels of space conditioning and climate control needed, "pull apart" the building and position architectural elements as participants in a more comprehensive ensemble. A minimal provisioning of shelter for many of the spaces was recognized as acceptable in this benign, Mediterranean-like climate, with a parasol as primary design intervention offering visitors sufficient protection from the intense summer sun and winter rains, and with smaller, more strictly conditioned exhibit "pavilions" nested underneath. Conceiving the project not as an object in a field but rather as an assemblage of "activity settings" in a spatial continuum including neighboring buildings and the tree-fringed meadow led to opportunities for energy and material savings *and* enriched experience. The notion of furnishing alleviated architecture as solely responsible for meeting all human wants and desires.

"Furnishing this larger room" is a compound of two presuppositions:
(1) assigning characteristics of rooms to presences in the landscape provides useful insight into the highly complex realm of the environment, and
(2) assigning characteristics of furnishings to larger built entities provides useful insight into the highly complex realm of architecture. Through an act of poetic association, insights are combined to produce a strikingly new (third) meaning.

Entailments associated with *architecture as furnishing a larger room* include:

- The environment comprises spaces that have room-like qualities.
- Outdoor rooms have the ability to provide some measure of comfort and protection.
- Architecture can be made up of sets of furnishings.
- One arranges sets of architectural elements in a room.
- Architectural elements may be repositioned according to user needs and ambient conditions.
- Architecture can be lightweight, perhaps portable.
- Architecture should be functional, ergonomic and comfortable.

"Room" motivates the designer, as an initial act, to observe, identify, and describe the size, complexity, orientation, materiality, structure, plumbing, and quality of light of the landscape spaces in which a project will be situated and in which it will be a part. These qualities have a profound ability to condition – shelter, screen, brighten, and envelop – the to-be-designed subspaces that will likely serve as the nexus of human activity. The earth, trees, and sky of this larger room are *analogous* to floor, walls, and ceiling *and* can assume these primary architectural roles. So recognizes Don Berry in his novel *Trask* in describing a Killamook settlement on the Oregon coast: "The rustle and papery whisper of firs formed a roof over the village."[5] Similarly, in Richard Leplastrier's Mapleton House in Queensland, "the surrounding trees form the true walls of

The spatiality of the landscape: room-like qualities in pre-existing settings inform architectural design inquiry.

the building."[6] The Mapleton House is shaped by and draws attention to preexisting conditions – a long curved walkway that connects workshop and main house also mediates an otherwise abrupt transition between forest and clearing, the site's two salient landscape features. The podium dwelling resides amidst the preexisting, screen-like walls and occupies the life zone between wet leaf-littered rainforest floor and raucous crowded canopy overhead.

Leplastrier's experiences working with Jørn Utzon on the Sydney Opera House in the 1960s and later living and working in Japan for two and a half years profoundly affect his ideas of architecture as graceful positioning of furnishings in a landscape room. Resources are not to be wasted, and yet resourcefulness and restraint are not incompatible with richness of effect and sophisticated performance. As philosopher Edward Casey observes: "The less material place is, the more powerful it becomes."[7]

Utzon and Leplastrier share an enthusiasm for the traditional Japanese house. To quote Utzon:

> The floor ... is a delicate bridge-like platform. This Japanese platform is like a tabletop. It is a piece of furniture ... here you have the feeling similar to the one you have when standing on a small wooden bridge, dimensioned just to take your weight and nothing more.[8]

Set nimbly atop the platform are vertical space-defining and conditioning elements such as *fusuma* and *shoji* partitions. Occupants replace these seasonally in response to changing ambient conditions, with lattice-clad partitions employed in summer to promote ventilation and thick rice-paper clad partitions installed in winter to trap heat while admitting light. These screens are moveable, removable, and vital to architectural function and manner.

Architect and educator Lars Bleher advocates for design expression residing at a scale between rooms and freestanding pieces of furniture.[9] "Built-ins" as arrangements in profile serve at the interface of stylistic human purposefulness and ambient forces. "Die Libelle" or "The Dragonfly," Behnisch and Partners' 1995 competition-winning proposal for a small open-air café adjacent to the Rathaus (City Hall) in the corner of Marktplatz in downtown Stuttgart, Germany, exemplifies the potency of this emphasis. The café as proposed is not positioned at the center of Marktplatz but at its edge, respecting and supporting patterns of traversing of the urban terrain, revealing awareness on the part of the design team of the larger, preexisting room, a roughly 250-foot-square plaza sharply defined by the contiguous façades of five- and six-story buildings, postwar replicas of medieval half-timbered structures that previously occupied the site. In the competition plan drawing, a colorful assemblage of round stools (one size) and round tables (two sizes) commands visual presence. Fixed elements such as walls, roofs, counters, and storage elements are drawn lightly and are not rendered. Absence of graphic weight parallels architectural dematerialization.

With Die Libelle, the light and provisional architecture recedes to the background to support what is primary to the life of a café in a public square in a major urban center. Such an assemblage of elements has, according to David Leatherbarrow: "The habit of disappearing when most vitally present, insofar as they are taken up or absorbed into the human body's various projects."[10]

Walls and dragonfly-wing-shaped roof elements slip past one another, blurring distinctions between interior and exterior space, while the informal configuration of drawn furnishings suggests mobility and impermanence, showing less the mark of the designer and rather the designs of others. The basic constellation of elements that is proposed allows for seemingly limitless adjustment in response to changing ambient conditions, individual comfort needs, and differences in group sizes and comportment of those frequenting the café.

Leplastrier extends this manner of thinking by assigning qualities of unpretentiousness, economy, lightness, and even portability and replaceability to elements typically considered primarily architectural. Furnishing-like building components such as window and bay assemblies, walls, partitions, and roof overhangs can be configured and modified to allow sensitive, comfort-providing adjustment in an elegantly purposeful way, expressing degrees of perceptivity commensurate with local environmental forces that are a primary impetus for construction. Thoughtfully located and flexible furnishing-like building elements serve as the interface between sheltering (built) and preexisting space, encouraging greater responsiveness to the surrounding room versus a distancing through sophisticated technologies of comfort-providing automation. While Kahn elevates the role of furnishings in the design of the Exeter Library, integrating desks with windows so that they merge into an overall building identity, with Leplastrier, "built" furnishings acquire expressive preeminence. They are the light footprint of the building itself.

Leplastrier's own pavilion-like one-room house in Lovett Bay, near Church Point north of Sydney, reveals both his passion for traditional Japanese building culture and his interest in "the concept of an adjustable house that can be attuned to climatic circumstances like a yacht adjusting to changes in the wind."[11] The lone, simple roof, extending beyond wall planes to shade interior space during the hot summer months, is offset by platforms of varying levels that define distinct settings yet preserve spatial continuity. The slight elevation change, one step as juncture of the pavilion and surrounding deck, is at once a seat and demarcation; a sectional jog that promises opportunities for repose and interaction while helping frame views of the Hawkesbury River and layers of bush-cloaked hills beyond. As with the Japanese house, vertical screens are minimal, light and flexible, providing a basic yet refined environmental control in the benign Mediterranean-like climate of southeastern Australia. The kitchen and privy are outside.

Notions of architecture-as-encampment and furnishings raise important questions about perceptions of boundedness and breadth of inhabitation. Mark Johnson describes a process by which our own containment as centered, embodied beings leads to identification of surrounding presences of containment:

> **We almost always superimpose a container schemata on our center–periphery orientation. Where we draw the bounding container will almost always depend on our purposes, interests, perceptual capacities, conceptual system, and values. But we tend to define both our physical and mental identities by virtue of their containment.**[12]

"Bounding" may be preferable to containment, as a boundary intimates orientation, threshold, and negotiation as much as divide and limit. What is important in Johnson's view is that it is possible to adjust conceptions of the breadth of this encircling and what is fundamental to its creation, such as with the notion of *architecture as furnishing this larger room*, where a built entity is less a divide and more a (porous) mediator between our selves and larger entities, rooms at once tremendously spatially complex and comforting in their bounding comprehensibility. The metaphor, and the work of Leplastrier informed by such an articulation, encourages radical reappraisal of situatedness: architectural furnishings, surfaces as bodily extensions and settings for gathering, are "outfoldings" toward a primary inhabitation, a horizon, an elliptical spatial field, a landscape under the stars. Within a "flux of awareness" lie simultaneously intimacy and close familiarity *and* a bounding ever-changingness of envelopment. The house, according to Deleuze and Guattari, "does not shelter us from cosmic forces; at most it filters and selects them."[13]

beyond

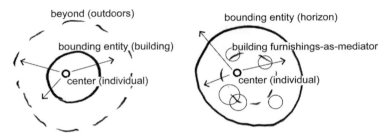

People perceive boundaries and containers in their environment. "Architecture-as-furnishing-this-larger-room" expands the scale of the boundary from building to horizon as primary envelopment.

Architecture-as-furnishings establishes resonances between postures of dwelling and presences in the landscape and corresponds vividly to David Leatherbarrow's reflections on "the topographical horizon of dwelling equipment" in his book *Uncommon Ground*:

> We begin to see that this corporeal schema is enmeshed within an expanding range of distances, a structured topography that includes where I am, which is to say where the things I now need are within reach, a middle distance, and an expansion towards the clear blue horizon; an equipmental, practical and environmental horizon. Not one of these can be separated from the others, hence the lateral spread of the ensemble that integrates these "rings" into one field, terrain or topography – the dining room, the street, and the town or landscape – differentiated but reciprocating.[14]

Furnishings are essential participants in this "lateral spread," drawing out continuities between the specific immediacy of embodied experience and mediations of a more expansive nature. The orientations of Leatherbarrow and Leplastrier indicate the inadequacy of philosopher Arnold Berleant's sharp distinction between participatory, "environmental," and neutrally distanced, picturesque aesthetics; instead, constant rhythmic succession of action and

Leatherbarrow's "equipmental, practical and environmental horizons."

reflection characterize the pragmatic aesthetics of human being.[15] Leplastrier's dictum *to furnish* helps sidestep picturesque/participatory and nature/culture dichotomies by intimating forms of environmental engagement residing in both the constitution of architecture and the manners of purposefulness and repose architectures engender. It offers a compelling means for viewing sustainable design as part of a larger trajectory, where quieter architectures facilitate a mutuality of inner and outer landscapes, and where poetry, experiential power, and "lightness" can be appreciated along with goals of resource efficiency and energy savings. Rich mutuality *is* building/project performance.

Leplastrier belongs to an informal group of Australian architects that includes Glenn Murcutt, Peter Stutchbury, and Lindsay Johnston, among others, who celebrate the formative potential of insightful landscape response in positioning architectural ensembles. Murcutt describes the experience of staying at Riversdale – next to the gallery site and annexed to the meadow room – as akin to camping.[16] Shed roofs meet and form a valley for collecting water for use in the spaces underneath. There is no heating system, the "hallway" between the sleeping quarters and the main meeting space is a covered verandah, open at its sides, and there are moveable elements throughout that enable generous linkages between interior and exterior space. Galvanized steel fins project beyond the building's west façade, providing afternoon shade. These fins house sliding doors that can be deployed to divide a four-person room in half. Within each sleeping space, an alcove pairs a bed with a window assembly that combines a room-width fixed light at bed height with hinged wooden shutters above. When the shutters are open, one has unobstructed access to breezes, light and framed views of the river (the river-as-frame mirrors and registers for the waking occupant the ambient conditions of the emerging day). Within the shutters are smaller framed screens that can be opened independently to allow natural ventilation and protection from insects (when the shutters are closed).

This simple constellation of built furnishings enables countless adjustments in response to changes in ambient conditions and inhabitant activity. As with so many of Murcutt's projects, visual expression depends on subtle manipulation and restrained detailing of the profile of the skin. Riversdale takes on Miesian clarity, yet Murcutt acknowledges and accommodates a great variety of local environmental factors as basic design necessity. This is a very different form of

Shade fins and window assemblies in typical bay of sleeping quarters, Arthur and Yvonne Boyd Art Centre, Riversdale, New South Wales, Australia (Glenn Murcutt in collaboration with Reg Lark and Wendy Lewin, 1996–1999).

reductivism than the Farnsworth House,[17] an arboreal economy of layers inducing the movement of air and the progressive lightening of elements as they move up and out toward light and sky.

William Kittredge offers stirring portrayals of prevailing narratives of the American West, a dimension of which pertains to how "ideas of paradise often involve a place to camp."[18] Riversdale, in the southeast Australian bush, is an earthly projection of camp-like paradise in which the temperate breezes and the damp chill of a rainy winter evening are cues to awareness within a cradling of meadow, river, hills, verandah, and sleeping porch. While Murcutt and Leplastrier work primarily in rural contexts and on smaller projects, Riversdale being a relatively large commission by their standards, this skill of direct environmental and landscape response to architectures warrants translating to more densely settled urban and urbanizing contexts. Philosopher Giorgio Agamben even argues that "camp" offers a more fitting descriptor for twenty-first-century urbanisms than "city."[19] While this rings of real and dire circumstances of marginalized elements of society living on the edge in squalor,

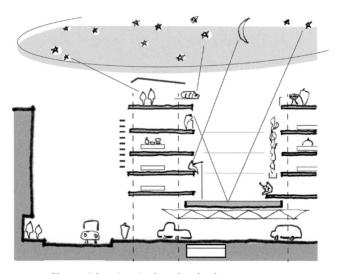

Encampment-like spatial settings in the urban landscape.

it can at the same time prompt proactive ways of thinking about the permanence of portions of building assemblies and the life of materials, primacy and openness of built-ins and screen-like skins, finely tuned adjustment of architectural "gear," and occupation of lantern-like space. Encampment-like platforms establish equipmental horizons; architectural instrumentation links immediacy of inhabitation to larger landscape events, living systems and evening sky. Projects as encampments are nodes within mega-encampments, at once enduring and transitional, stable and undergoing constant change.

If the city is aggregate and ensemble of innumerable hearths, localized place-making is in turn a precipitate of a region, the concentrate of compounds. Philosopher Edward Casey highlights Heidegger's identification of rooms obtaining from regions:

> **Heidegger's contribution to this history (of place) is to make room such a mediatrix expressly by virtue of the ingrediency of region, whose amplitude and dynamism make possible the generation of place and space alike. For the effect of region is the creation of the very spatiality (*Räumlichkeit*: literally, "roomliness") from which place is precipitated and space discerned.**[20]

Landscape rooms acquire their features and contours from the regional landscapes in which they are situated. With discerning insight, the architect furnishes rooms. The ensemble of furnishings, by virtue of its arrangement, invites imaginative extension out to encompassing profiles of the settings of dwelling and to innumerable worlds beyond. As Terry Eagleton describes in his own paraphrasing of Heidegger: "And it could never be grasped as a whole, trailing off as it does out of the corners of our vision, suggesting an infinity of possible connections beyond any horizon."[21]

Notes

1 Snyder 1990, 112.
2 Calvino 1992, 16.
3 *The American Heritage Dictionary; Second College Edition* 1982.

4 Architects Lindsay Johnston, Richard Leplastrier, and Peter Stutchbury assisted Glenn Murcutt in the 2001 Glenn Murcutt Master Class. Participants (including the author) spent the first week of the course at the Arthur and Yvonne Boyd Art Centre at Riversdale, West Cambewarra, New South Wales, designed by Murcutt in collaboration with Reg Lark and Wendy Lewin (1996–1999). Student teams were asked to design an art gallery at the meadow site a few hundred feet from Riversdale. The property, former estate of Australian painter Arthur Boyd, was given in trust to the people of Australia; the proposed gallery will house Boyd's work. For information on the class, see www.ozetecture.org.

5 Berry 2004, 235.

6 Spence 1998, 72.

7 Casey 1997, 90.

8 Frampton 1995, 247. The quote is taken from Utzon's article "Platforms and Plateaus: The Ideas of a Danish Architect," *Zodiac* (1962).

9 Lars Bleher was a member of the University of Oregon Architecture Department faculty, 2005–2010.

10 Leatherbarrow 2000, 157.

11 Spence 1998, 70.

12 Johnson 1987, 125.

13 Deleuze and and Guattari 1994, 182.

14 Leatherbarrow 2000, 66.

15 See Berleant 1992.

16 Glenn Murcutt explained the project as such during 2001 Master Class discussions.

17 Mies van der Rohe's 1951 house in Plano, IL, a masterwork of high modernism: www.farnsworthhouse.org.

18 Kittredge 2000, 173.

19 See Agamben 1998.

20 Casey 1997, 252.

21 Eagleton 1990, 288–289.

CHAPTER 7

Landscapes and Machines

Ideas of architecture as landscape's precipitate, analog, and generative force weave about the legacy of projections of the body as metaphorical prompt. Because notions of landscape have transformed over time, so have approaches to architecture intended to acknowledge it. A trajectory of meanings in art, philosophy, and science proceeds from attitudes of landscape as the site of intensive interrogation and distanced aesthetic contemplation, to a view of landscape within the framework of systems (and ecosystems) theory, to poststructuralist critiques of ideas of nature and emerging interest in environmental aesthetics as embodied engagement carrying ethical significance.

Noteworthy today is the tremendous popularity of landscape metaphors, the diversity of intentions that drive architects to appropriate the landscape, and avoidance of claims of universality that characterizes postmodern thinking. Why are landscape metaphors so important to recent generations of architects, and in what ways do they direct design inquiry? With a goal of environmental sensitivity and resourcefulness, it would seem inherently advantageous that architects look beyond buildings to the landscape in deriving conceptual organizational strategies. Certain types of landscape metaphor appear to motivate particularly nuanced, attuned environmental readings and foster productive collaborative inquiry.

David Miller of the Miller/Hull Partnership finds conceptual opportunities inherent to dynamic architecture/landscape relationships more sustaining of interest than isolated objects of aesthetic speculation.[1] Ken Radtkey, principal of Blackbird Architects in Santa Barbara, California:

> **Sought the definitions of landscape and architecture, and found little essential separation between the two. Definitions of landscape center around vistas and viewing spaces ... perhaps the notion of garden.[2]**

The garden occupies "the heart of architecture" in Radtkey's work, offering as it does an ideal fusion of natural integrity and thoroughly artful execution. Many are the attractions in such richly textured environments.

Along these lines, it is precisely the *variability and pliability* of the landscape, its myriad guises and thick defiance of one encompassing definition, which explain its limitlessness as metaphorical source. For David Cook, formerly a partner with Behnisch, the landscape is a recurring source of inspiration as:

> It is infinitely variable and non-static; is ever changing, responding to local conditions, ebbs and flows of the seasons, cycles of nature. The landscape serves to stimulate all of the senses. Numerous buildings, in contrast, are rather stagnant. Reference to the landscape also offers us a degree of freedom, as we are obviously all rather reluctant to acknowledge too many buildings as sources of inspiration![3]

Cook's view resonates with Latour and Yaneva's drawing of correspondences between architectures and dynamic living systems:

> A building project resembles much more a complex ecology than it does a static object in Euclidean space. As many architects and architectural theorists have shown, biology offers much better metaphors for speaking about buildings.[4]

Architect Vincent James builds narratives where architectural proposals, subject to certain environmentally sensitive rules or laws, emerge from lively processes of unfolding, and where the role of the architect is that of "orchestrating, channeling, organizing, and filtering the temporal phenomena of the built environment."[5] The design team imposes theses rules as methodological bracketing devices, whether they are meteorological, geological, biological, ecological, or hydrological in nature. A project becomes a setting in motion and eventual settling of spatial (architectural) presences triggered by forces and disruptions such as erosion, channeling, deposition, etc. A process can play out again and again, with the same laws underlying generative forces yet with varying intensities causing different formations upon stabilization. A conceptual operation as creative interpretation of ever-emergent biophysical patterns can have profound physical effects.

Emulation or interaction?

In our paper, "Landscape Metaphors, Ecological Imperatives and Architectural Design," Kaarin Knudson and I examine a limited cross-section of contemporary projects and attempt a grouping of different metaphorical appropriations of the landscape.[6] There appear to be two basic metaphorical types, one that puts focus on emulation of qualities of the landscape and one that places emphasis on the manner in which buildings interact with their surroundings. While no sharp categorical line separates the two approaches, the distinction is useful in revealing implications of manner of appropriation.

In an emulative approach, a landscape feature or environmental phenomenon informs metaphorically the character and/or behavior of a work of architecture. In some instances a project operates as formal and spatial analog to local topography, as with the park-like built terrain that distinguishes Foreign Office Architect's Yokohama International Port Terminal. In some instances building performance and emulative expression align seamlessly, as with sun-shading and light-distributing devices on the roof of Renzo Piano's Menil Collection in Houston that were "immediately christened a 'leaf.' "[7] Similarly, Behnisch and Partners conceptualized the Plenarsaal in the Bundestag in Bonn as gathering under a tree in a meadow, an apt vision for an inclusively democratic modern society. This notion informed the design of the light-diffusing roof assembly above the main assembly chamber.

Will Bruder and Partners' Burton Barr Central Library in Phoenix, an outcrop akin to formations in the surrounding Sonoran desert topography, marries spatial richness and stellar environmental performance. Conceptualized as a "crystal canyon," the library's reading, book collection, and various public spaces are sandwiched between shade providing thickened spatial elements to the east and west that contain stairs, offices, restrooms, mechanical chases, etc.

Plenarsaal, World Conference Center, Bonn (formerly Bundestag): democratically elected representatives gather "under a tree" (under a layered roof assembly that diffuses light in a manner akin to the foliage of a tree) (Behnisch and Partners).

These more "closed" portions of the building shade in a manner similar to the walls of desert slot canyons. An array of horizontal fins on the south façade and fabric "sails" on the north shade in the early morning and late afternoon in summer. These prevent overheating and protect the collection, offering a practical and elegant passive solution suited to a hot, arid setting and an internal load-dominated building type such as a library. In addition, "candlelight" column caps in the double height reading space at the top level "catch" direct sunlight penetrating skylights during the summer solstice.

Alex Wyndham's "Deciduous House," a residential infill prototype for alley lots in Eugene, Oregon, responds to environmental stimuli in a manner attuned poetically to one of the region's salient landscape features. Oaks undergo processes of transformation – budding, leafing, shedding – tied to seasonal change. These stages of the life of an oak manifest in turn dramatically different luminous, thermal, and spatial microenvironments. With "Deciduous House," south-facing insulated wall "leaves" fold upward in summer to become trellis-like shade screens that filter light from above. Sudden and spacious generosity mirrors summer brightness of cloudless skies and glowing smiles of passersby feeling the sun's warmth for the first time in months.

In winter mode vectors of influence reverse, trellises contract and turn to walls, and the dwelling becomes snugly introspective, surrounded by silent matte gray light, gentle rain, and black wet limbs. January dimness counterbalances the light exuberance of summer; the world closes in, paralleling the inhabitants' introspection. Resonant with Tanizaki's observation, darkness is more than blackness and consists of countless gradients, from tangible opacity of surfaces to endless depth of space.[8] Visual cues gain in subtlety as acoustic sensitivity amplifies.

An emulative approach is the very basis of *biomimicry*, with nature serving as the primary source domain for innovation in the creation of products, projects,

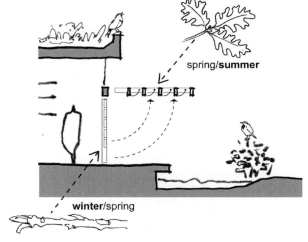

"Deciduous House": buildings expand and contract to reflect changes in the seasons and our moods. The idea of a "deciduous house" derives from Alex Wyndham's Master of Architecture advanced level design studio project (2006).

and systems. Given its graceful resourcefulness, simple appearance often belying tremendous physical and structural sophistication, and the foreignness of the concept of waste, nature serves as a most logical basis of artifice.[9] In many discussions of *biomimicry* focusing on the landscape, variable and non-static attributes are emphasized, rather than capacity to invoke quiet contemplation or inspire abstracted geometric patterns. Built landscapes emulating those found in nature might be event-laden, dynamic yet supportive, characterized by complex beauty and ambient richness, and realized with great material and energy efficiency.

In comparison to an emulative approach, a work of architecture might interact directly and possibly become "fused with the landscape," as with the Nelson-Atkins Museum Addition in Kansas City by Steven Holl Architects.[10] Interactive metaphors can prompt designers to consider ecological and climatic subtleties of site and environs so as to develop organizational schemas where building elements and landscape elements operate closely and at many levels. For its winning design for the Hostler Recreation Center at the American University of Beirut (2003–2007), Vincent James Associate Architects defied competition parameters by dividing the building mass into several smaller pieces, a strategy enabling "horizontal migration" of shaded outdoor plazas and the creation of "landscape drifts." The project, taking advantage as it does of cooling afternoon sea breezes, is choreography of built form, landscape, climate, and the complex social life of the university community.[11]

As with many of his projects, Alvar Aalto's library at Mount Angel Seminary (1970) acts as a *couplet* that augments awareness of contrasts of surrounding landscape rooms by embedding their distinct characters in an architectural progression. One-story rectilinear volumes reinforce the spatial structure of the seminary's hilltop quadrangle to the south. In contrast, the fluidly organic reading space opens to the sky while stepping down toward and framing views of the mixed agricultural/forested landscape to the north. Block-like forms as extensions of the geometry of the adjacent quad act as threshold and foil in preparation for focused study in concert with glimpses of forest, farms, and the vault of clouds merging at the distant horizon.

With Blackbird Architects' "Casa Nueva" offices in Santa Barbara, a three-story, freestanding "living" trellis immediately adjacent to the building provides an armature for the growth of vines and a configuration of cloth shades. The "rigging and sails" mediate between workspaces and a suburban, freeway-dominated context, filtering noise and pollutants and providing nest sites for birds. A blossoming green billboard along with garden courts on the protected side of the building are primary figures of order and expression that add playful variety and functional complexity to an economical, box-like volume of offices.[12]

Canyon, deciduous tree, drift, couplet, rigging: emulative and interactive examples suggest how a metaphor is an expression of and prompt for an architecture acquiring fuller resolution through conception of its incompletion and the nature of its participation in a greater totality. A project can operate both as analog and intensifier of its surroundings, providing conjecture and offering a specific device for ways in which, to quote Ken Radtkey, "spatial, visual, physical, and more complex environmental connections may re-sensitize us to our world."[13] Promising architectures of landscape assimilation and accommodation follow from an approach where biomimicry is a dimension of a larger endeavor to integrate building and natural systems processes that may involve recall, feedback, offset, transposition, facilitation, or harmonization.

Architectures as interactive, embedded systems

Tracing the life of metaphorical and ecological thinking in the highly celebrated California Academy of Sciences (CAS) in Golden Gate Park in San Francisco adds perspective on correspondences between initial conceptualizations and the "realities" of engaging environmental issues in architecture. Frank Almeda, CAS' Director of Biology, recounts the process that led to awarding the commission to Renzo Piano Building Workshop.[14] Unlike several other architects vying for the job, Piano did not offer a conceptual design proposal during the interview process and instead spent time observing the site and its surroundings. He then generated a loose and evocative section sketch of an undulating roofscape mimicking the surrounding San Francisco hills. A parasol-like extension of local topography, the enveloping green or "living" roof also offered a direct, poetic

Renzo Piano Building Workshop's California Academy of Sciences as formal and functional analog to the hills surrounding San Francisco's Golden Gate Park.

means of reducing the urban heat island effect, moderating temperature extremes within the building through processes of thermal stratification, retaining rainwater on site, and sheltering exhibit and other spaces below.

Paul Kephart of the ecological design firm Rana Creek was hired to configure and install the 160,000-square-foot living roof. Kephart's interest is "moving beyond evocation" and in creating projects that "take on the function of demonstrating ecological contribution."[15] He recognized the tremendous potential of an undulating roofscape supporting living trays of differing aspects and orientations. North-facing, shady, and relatively moist patches would stand out against those facing south and subject to greater levels of insolation; steep portions of the roof would contrast those of a gentler grade. Microclimatic and topographic variation would support a level of biological diversity far greater than the flat, "extensive," and more common moss sedum roofs.

Due to unique project circumstances, most notably the involvement of Paul Kephart and Rana Creek and a scientifically sophisticated client team, the conception of the CAS evolved in its relationship with the surrounding environment from one motivated primarily by emulation of landscape form and more circumscribed understandings of interactive performance to one that emulates *and* interacts with the landscape in highly intentional, ecologically beneficial, and dynamically evolving ways. In the end, Rana Creek incorporated a "diverse assemblage of indigenous plants," 50 species altogether.[16] An institution dedicated to advancing knowledge of natural history and science gathers under a constructed landscape that powerfully projects its mission and serves as test-bed for education and experimentation.

Rana Creek's participation in CAS is part of a more comprehensive endeavor to configure buildings so they can contribute demonstrably to a broader ecological function. In several projects living roofs serve as nurseries for native and threatened plant species such as grasses and wildflowers. Plant communities in turn provide habitats for native invertebrate populations. Insects attract birds making their way up and down continental flyways. An urban building becomes a stopover linked to hemispheric scale migration!

Rana Creek participated in the design of the Transbay Center Terminal in downtown San Francisco. Transbay's 5.4-acre living roof is intended to function as much-needed open space that also shelters a complex interchange of mass transit systems underneath. A rooftop constructed wetland garden performs polishing treatment of graywater, saving money and resources. Additionally, rooftop habitats reference California ecosystems. As with other projects Rana Creek is involved in, innovation results from scrutiny of the impact of internal building dynamics on immediate surroundings. If building functions require rejection of moisture, heat, or other forms of waste, opportunities are sought to capture these as resources and put them to work elsewhere in the building or in the development of exterior microecologies; a roof serves to shelter, collect, and redistribute nutrients and provide didactic links to a broader reality in the heart of a bustling city. This perspective affirms a dimension of ecological design pursued in previous chapters. Works of architecture become components of viable urban ecologies, life-enhancing and resourcefully abundant systems embedded in and interacting with others of greater magnitude.

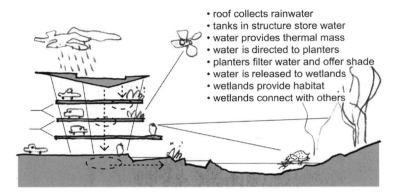

- roof collects rainwater
- tanks in structure store water
- water provides thermal mass
- water is directed to planters
- planters filter water and offer shade
- water is released to wetlands
- wetlands provide habitat
- wetlands connect with others

Works of architecture as assemblages of systems embedded in others of greater magnitude.

An understanding of architecture as stimulating and building ecologies resonates with Ricoeur's notion of metaphor:

> To present all things *"as in act"* – such could well be the *ontological* function of metaphorical discourse, in which every dormant potentiality of existence appears *as* blossoming forth, every latent capacity for action *as* actualized.[17]

Focus on particular ecological conditions points not to the superfluousness of metaphors but instead highlights their provisional character, where what unfolds forces a reevaluation or evolution of a concept in the act of making. A process that interweaves ecological opportunity and metaphor as imaginative extension can produce new understandings that will likely be instilled in the pre-conceptual register of subsequent undertakings.

A machine is a landscape for living in

In embracing the landscape (ecological), Lakoff and Johnson might discourage the outright abandonment of the metaphor of the machine, the paradigmatic qualifier of architecture in the twentieth century. Certainly there is a measure of "rightness" to a machine-like characterization of architecture given the manner in which architectures are produced, the efficiencies and levels of performance expected, and the technologies that projects consist of and house. Of interest are the entailments ordinarily associated with the machine metaphor and how the conceptual system alters when coupled with ideas of architectures of landscape.

When Le Corbusier made this famous proclamation that "a house is a machine for living in," he not only captured the exuberance felt toward the cool rationality of industrialization in the 1920s; he also directed a primary line of inquiry amongst architects for the remainder of the twentieth century.[18] Through invocation and confirmation of the metaphor, Le Corbusier both unapologetically acknowledged a reality – the architect's increasing distance from hand-based craft and necessary engagement with industrial modes of production – and motivated design culture at large to confirm fervently this new reality. Entailments that made Le Corbusier's metaphor *the house is a machine for living in* so powerful in transforming ideas about the design of the house include:

- A house is rationally organized.
- A house is appreciated for its spare elegance and utility.
- A house is the result of industrial manufacturing processes.
- A house is made from machine-like materials.
- A house is self-contained, "complete," like a body-as-machine (distinct from its environment).
- The components of a house fulfill human activities in a highly utilitarian, machine-like manner.
- Parts of a house can be replaced periodically to ensure its continued function.

Le Corbusier's dictum, as well as his cleanly ordered, taut-skinned, early residential work, affirm the modernist separation of nature and culture in discourse and their troubled entanglement in practice. Inattention is a form of appropriation, expressive autonomy the other side of a house as nexus of powerfully intertwined, resource-intensive nature–culture networks. For Latour, the moderns are:

going to be able to make nature intervene at every point in the fabrication of their societies while they go right on attributing to nature its radical transcendence; they are going to be able to become the only actors in their own political destiny while they go right on making their society hold together by mobilizing nature.[19]

For Latour, once society makes explicit the proliferation of nature/culture hybrids, tracks more carefully their influence, and admits incapacity to understand them fully, it embraces a "non-modern" project of guarded and liberated conscientiousness.

Architectures will always be projections of bodies, concentrators and extensions of landscapes, and types of machines. Within a relational context, an appropriately non-modern notion of the architectural machine would be that of prosthetic components, coordinated arrays of devices positioned within larger "eco-social-technical" assemblages in the service of life. This would appear to be at the heart of Smout Allen's "Augmented Landscapes" or the work of Behnisch and Partners, where a conscious arranging of stock (machined) parts is

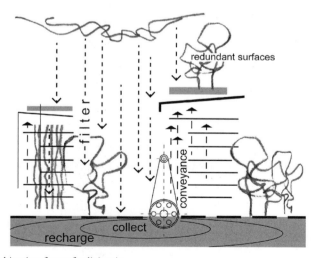

A machine is a forest for living in.

not an aesthetic end but is instead an enabler of expressive events, as when the hand and the handrail couple.

In exploring hybrid metaphors that associate life, the body, and the machine, metaphors nuanced and diverse in their accommodation, designers might take a cue from the organic–inorganic "arrangements" Deleuze and Guattari develop in their work. They eschew ideas of the body and human identity as singular, and rather conceive individuals as constellations of multiplicities of diverse influence, with any one singular identity capable of establishing "blocks of becoming" with entities that lie beyond, including entities with machine-like or otherwise inorganic qualities. Deleuze and Guattari argue: "It is no longer even appropriate to group biological, physiochemical, and energetic intensities on the one hand, and mathematical, aesthetic, linguistic, informational, semiotic intensities, etc., on the other."[20] Instead they speak of event-laden active processes and the sensations thus generated: "vibrating sensation – coupling sensation – opening or splitting, hollowing out sensation."[21] Articulations of such sensations as a formative design motivation may offer a promising path for creating architectures as animated mechanisms sophisticated in their behavior, supportive of life, and expressive of their technical and biological constitution.

Acknowledging artifice at work in imagining architectures as support for the replenishment of nature, alchemic metaphorical concoctions might be derived from notions discussed previously: non-equilibrium ecosystems and disturbances, ecological markets, collapsing of function and stacking of value, deadwood, architectural furnishings, non-static gardens, prosthetics, and arrangements of sensations. Whatever the specific commingling, desirable entailments associated with a successful metaphor would suggest:

- interaction and incompleteness: need for broader-scale connectivity as resolution of site-scale architectural identity;
- lightness: encampment-like architectural character and/or prosthetic-like intervening;
- incongruence, or playful association of the dissimilar, for instance the organic and inorganic and the biological and technical;

- dynamism and uncertainty, where a project is a setting up of processes that enhance natural systems' function over time, such that it provides ongoing opportunities for learning and discovery (Gross would call for a "metaphor that suggests the unplannable in nature"[22]);
- verticality: stacking, overlapping, and fitting out;
- transdisciplinarity as conceptual and territorial renegotiation.

Sample metaphors that intimate certain of these entailments include:

- flights and perchings along a green frame;
- dispersing conduits;
- peninsular interdigitation;
- networks buffering cores;
- folds monitoring waterpockets;
- scaffolds of matrices and cores;
- embroidered pleats in green wedges;
- green fabric incubation;
- moraine gardens amidst a braided stream;
- solar orchards;
- civic ecosystems marketplaces.

Several of these borrow directly from operative concepts in landscape ecology. "Dispersing conduits," for example, derives from the concept of a dispersal corridor. Others combine philosophical and landscape ecological notions, as with "flights and perchings along a green frame" that links Dewey's birdlike articulation of human activity with a concept of a "network of green space for an urban area."[23] Similarly, "embroidered pleats in green wedges" compounds Gilles Deleuze's cloth-like metaphor of continuous fold as the archetype of baroque sensibility with an ecological concept for a landscape structure that "keeps developed areas apart while bringing greenspace closer to the heart of settlement."[24]

Honoring Ricoeur's faith in metaphor's potency, trial-like combinations instigate productive design speculation: building bioreserves, billboard aviaries,

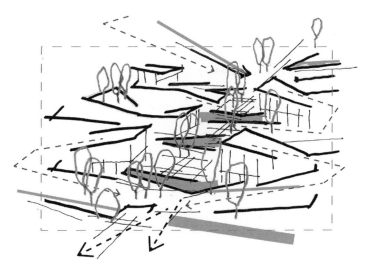

"Folds along waterpockets" as constructed expressions of architectural, landscape architectural, and ecological relationships.

water-collecting slot canyon avenues and office parks, weak-formed built deltas, stormwater nurseries, riparian processors, upland savannah commons, urban housing forests, (real time) intelligent avian rooftops. Such immaterial (re)characterizations could matter in fashioning built landscapes of regenerative potential.

Notes

1   This is a paraphrasing of David Miller's comments during a lecture sponsored by the Department of Architecture at the University of Oregon, May 7, 2007.

2   Personal correspondence with Ken Radtkey, July 27, 2007.

3   Personal correspondence with David Cook, July 18, 2007.

4   Latour and Yaneva 2008, 89.

5   James and Yoos 2006, 67.

6   See Knudson and Muller 2009. In the paper, Knudson and I make a
    further distinction within each type between emulative metaphors that are
    "formal" and those that are "dynamic," and interactive metaphors that are
    "generic" and those that are "specific."
7   Piano 1997, 80.
8   See Tanizaki 1977.
9   See Benyus 1997.
10 Zacks 2007, 101.
11 James and Yoos 2006.
12 See: www.bbird.com/projects/places-to-work/apc.
13 Personal correspondence with Ken Radtkey, July 27, 2007.
14 The description comes from a conversation with Frank Alameda during a
    visit to the CAS construction site on January 19, 2008.
15 Personal correspondence with Paul Kephart, January 2008.
16 See: www.ranacreek.com/projects/california-academy-of-science.
17 Ricoeur 1977, 43 (italics original).
18 See Shepard 1998, 96: "For hunter/gatherers the living metaphor of cosmic
    power is other species; for farmers it is the mother; for pastoralists, the
    father; for urban peoples, it has become the machine."
19 Latour 1993, 32.
20 Deleuze and Guattari 1987, 109.
21 Deleuze and Guattari 1994, 168.
22 Gross 2003, 38.
23 See Hellmund and Smith 2006, 2–3.
24 See Deleuze 1993 for discussion of baroque sensibility and a continuous
    fold; quote is from Hellmund and Smith 2006, 3.

Part III

Ecoarchitectural Strategies and Orders

CHAPTER 8

Networks

Presuppositions of the discreteness of building and landscape systems affect partnership structures and the views of commitments and obligations that architects seek. Daniel Solomon critiques the distinctively "modernist scheme of things" that liberates architects from obligation other than that of the design of buildings (and only certain aspects of buildings at that, as Latour's nature–culture indicates).[1] In critiquing this isolation of responsibility, urbanists and architectural theorists lament the incoherence of overall form and its consequences for legibility and the social life of the city, and the ecological fragmentation this perspective contributes to.

Philosopher Edward Casey maintains: "By 'strung out between wilderness and site,' I mean that we drastically lack viable and significant intermediate positions between these two extremities."[2] In realizing projects that act as nature/culture intermediaries of the kind Casey believes would benefit contemporary culture so profoundly, environmental scientists, biologists, architects, landscape architects, artists, planners, policy-makers, activists, and others are called upon to tease out incongruities, identify connections, and honor tensions between realms of environmental health and architectural quality. The structuring of collaborative relationships prefigures tendril-like structuring of space. Through ecological engagement, notions of order, space-making, proportions, and other issues designers traditionally contend with do not disappear; instead, they evolve.

Hans-Georg Gadamer suggests: "Discourse that is intended to reveal something requires that the thing be broken open by the question."[3] Questions introduced by exposure to urban ecological concerns break the resolute "thingness" of architecture and suggest new diagrams of collaboration illustrative of redistribution of emphasis and refashioning of professional relationships in different phases of design. L'OEUF in Montreal, Mithun in

Seattle, and Hass Cook Zemmrich in Stuttgart, to name only a few firms, embrace next-generation integrated design models in which contracts are devised to allow broad interdisciplinary teams prolonged interaction in preliminary phases in order to develop a shared yet malleable project vision. Narratives generated incorporate performance goals for building–landscape systems interaction and alleviate conflicts during later phases when changes are cumbersome and costly.

In a more subversive model of participation, ecologist and designer Paul Kephart describes the native plant nurseries his firm Rana Creek incorporates on green roofs as acts of "ecosabotage."[4] Motivated by the biologically productive potential of the city, Kephart leads an activist, "protest" consultancy operating in reaction to the ecological indifference of architects and their formalist preoccupations. When an architect envisions a white blossoming roof in recollection of a time when seabirds once flocked to a site, Kephart establishes a rooftop ecology that encourages the seabirds' return.

Working on projects at the intersection of art, architecture, and natural science, aware of and endeavoring to move beyond the competing orientations and goals of participants working within the diverse teams he assembles, artist Michael Singer directs initial environmental design emphasis to smaller-scale elements, spaces of charged occasion at the intersection of indoor and outdoor rooms, biology, art, architecture, and culture.[5] After developing several of these "place-moments," the team next stitches these into a comprehensive site-scale armature. Singer's collaborative design provocations require diverse input that produces a disarming effect and creates intimacy within a team that has become, according to Gross, a "new society in nature based on the experimental self-organization of its members."[6] Focus on a project-scale move as inaugural endeavor shifts to emphasis on rituals of encounter with entities and beings free to enter and exit designed frames. The installation at Denver International Airport Concourse C is an example of such a structuring; the palette of textured concrete, vegetation, and birds contrasts memorably with the ubiquity of aluminum cladding and chainstore signage found in air terminals.

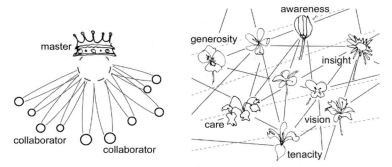

The master coordinator (Echinacea cone head) model of architectural practice gives way to skillful, garden-like communities.

The poet Gary Snyder praises the horizontality of a model like this where "Membership in a work association ... is a membership in a network. Networks cut across communities with their own kind of territoriality, analogous to the long migrations of geese and hawks."[7]

In the context of a robust collaborative network of high-frequency feedback, architects retain coordinating roles through constant repositioning. Architectural theorist and educator Howard Davis describes a dynamic, rotational image of relationships of participants where the location of those with deep expertise in one area, that of architects for example, shifts by degrees from a vertical to a more lateral orientation and back, in order that specialized knowledge can settle and be upset again during the course of design ideation and in subsequent project phases. Consistent with this, Edinburgh-based architect Malcolm Fraser offers an approachable and contextually saturated model of practice as a means to maintain confident humility. Fraser becomes a storyteller of his native city; his projects in turn invite passage to events along waterways and in the dense labyrinth of alleyways of the Old Town.[8] The stance offers more versatility than the figure caught inescapably in a chain-bound *dynamic d'enfer* (dynamic from hell) cut by Rem Koolhaas.[9]

Embedding ecology in most basic statements of design intention

Addressing the hellishness that is the world's sixth mass extinction, a collaborative structure of an ecological nature would lead to malleable formulations of design purpose that combine biological and constructed domains. Habitat elements, connectivity goals, stormwater management requirements, and potential choreographies between human and nonhuman activities suggest the value of *a statement of goals and intentions for urban ecological design and management*, versus a more circumscribed "problem definition statement," as a productive articulation of collaborative intent, one driven by a goal of intervention as environmental betterment (vs. design as avoidance of harm). In recognition of Randolph Hester's insight that "spatial specificity allows for ecological intervention," a statement of this nature would locate emphasis within a spectrum of (ecological) possibility a project team would proceed within.[10] In some instances, it suffices to articulate broader spatial parameters for certain habitat types and landscape ecological structures, for example recommendations for width, number, and continuity of green corridors linking adjacent patches of habitat. In other cases, ecologist–designer teams may have confidence to incorporate specific needs of species in project planning.

Matching habitat and development types

Relative to the countless life-worlds of nonhuman species, cities exhibit structural uniformity: hard ground surfaces and raised vertical masses (blocky buildings) akin to rock outcrops. Urban environments attract shelf-nesting birds and other species with spatial requirements suited to these basic profiles, and yet are unfit for many others. The biologist Michael Rosenzweig encourages designers to "diversify the habitats of our surroundings instead of creating, as we now do, the very limited number of habitat architectures that we have come to like."[11] An aggressive urban ecological design requires establishment of heterogeneous mosaics of built/urban morphologies to meet the needs of a greater number of species. A greater formal diversity and structural complexity, from the scale of weeps to building façades and

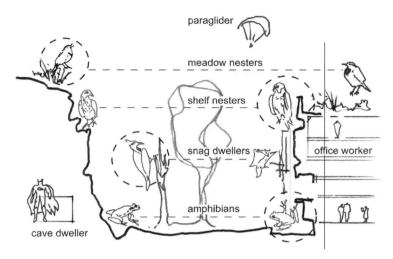

Built habitat structures paralleling heterogeneity in the natural landscape.

small-scale outdoor rooms to the patterning of urban blocks, could promote biodiversity goals in a manner that would contribute to phenomenal experience, awareness, and delight.

Historical and current ecological conditions, alterations of a site and its context over time, connections to other sites and barriers to movement, spatial/structural diversity, ambient light levels, etc.: these factors shape consideration of present opportunity and prospects for a more diverse future. One dimension of the initial design phase entails breakdown of characteristics of habitat types, biotic/abiotic formations defined by dominant plant communities, prevailing climate, soils, disturbance regimes, etc., that may exist on or near the site or may have done so in the past. A subsequent speculation pertains to how desired and functional attributes of these types may be incorporated in a design intervention, itself a pattern of disturbance and morphological alteration. In her master of landscape architecture thesis, "Biodiversity and the City: Habitat Integrated Architecture in the Urban Landscape" (2008), Shannon McGinley engages in this speculation and offers a methodology for identifying congruities between possible habitat features and development components.[12] McGinley's investigation speaks to the habitat potential of open space portions of a site as well as the ecological potential of building elements.

Ecologist Robert MacArthur observes that diversity of bird species in a given area "is largely determined by the structural features of the habitat" (regardless of the number of plant species present).[13] Subsequent research builds on MacArthur's understanding that spatial structure influences likelihood of colonization. Biologist and plant ecologist Jeremy Lundholm refers to these physical parameters as habitat templates.[14] Working with these templates, designers might ask what configurations ordinarily included in project development – a building skin/wall assembly that forms a thermal envelope, a roof that protects from the elements, a crevasse that acts as a conduit for moving water – might, if modified perhaps only slightly, double (or quintuple) in purposefulness by offering surrogate habitat. A development incorporating "extensive" green roofs might approximate the behavior of an upland prairie in terms of plant communities, soil structure, moisture content, and solar exposure, and therefore provide homes for imperiled ground-nesting birds who rely on these conditions to raise their offspring. This effort is not restoration as re-creation of an ideal set of attributes but a speculative act of spatial transposition, an open experiment with future biological possibility. In working with habitat types and exploring a meshing of needs, designers might begin to imagine new architectural possibilities: housing forests, urban recreational wetlands (fens for people in summer and amphibians in winter?), buildings as riparian slot canyons.

Designing for species

An ecologically supportive patterning of builtscapes and landscape infrastructures – hard, soft, gray, and green – relies on informed judgment as to when to encourage crossings between habitat boundaries and when to sharpen these distinctions, for example between core human habitat and core nonhuman habitat of specialist species. In the process the requirements of certain groupings of species, worth investigating in their own right, can suggest a broader envelope of parameters of spatial structure within which the needs of numerous other species can be accommodated. In a manner akin to aligning

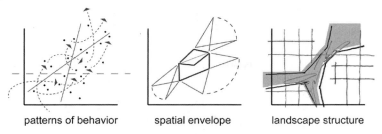

| patterns of behavior | spatial envelope | landscape structure |

Species behavior and movement suggest broader habitat-based spatial parameters.

development features with habitat types, designers and ecologists can create inventories of potential nonhuman inhabitant needs, that is, species-based "client briefs," and speculate as to their viability given the type and likely morphology of the project in question.

Rosenzweig asks design teams to give careful consideration to the life histories of species:

> Shrike reconciliation ecology teaches us some general lessons. First, drink deeply from the natural history of the species you want to help. Study their reproductive cycles, their diets, and their behavior. Abstract the essence of their needs from what you observe. Then apply it without worrying whether your redesign of the human landscape will resemble a wilderness. It won't, so feel free to be outrageously creative. Birds and other animals appreciate abstract art more than you think.[15]

By gaining sufficient understanding of the numbers, spatial needs, migratory patterns, threats to be avoided, and numerous other factors that affect the life histories of the species in question, designers are positioned to devise stages, steps, levels, and niches that facilitate their occupation of urban landscapes. This approach must be set within a broader recognition that there are innumerable species a design team could plan for, many with highly uncertain futures. To that end, cognizant of the formidable practical and philosophical challenges inherent to the effort, Cerra, McGinley, and I attempt criteria for determining what species to consider as part of project development in our paper "Building an Arc: Architecture, Biodiversity and the City." The following is a summary of the factors we discuss:

Species contribution to larger ecosystem function

Certain "linchpin" or "sentinel" species, for example Oregon White Oak in the Pacific Northwest, offer value by providing habitat components for numerous others. As Oregon white oak habitat has dwindled due to its suitability for other forms of development (approximately 80 percent has disappeared from the Willamette Valley since the arrival of settlers in the mid-nineteenth century) so have the numbers of denizens who depend on it, hundreds of species endemic to the bioregion. Incorporating patches of oak in project site development, whether as part of larger woodland, savanna, or prairie habitats, may positively impact resource availability, reproduction success and other survival factors for many species residents.

Species sensitivity/edge tolerance

Some species, certain migratory birds for example, are highly sensitive to noise, light, and other stressors. Because they are subject to "edge effect"[16] and require core habitat and buffer, they would not likely occupy spaces with significant human presence.[17] Other species have more moderate levels of sensitivity, and awareness of their unique needs could lead to creative design stratification. Projects might be zoned spatially along a gradient from intensive habitat to intensive (human) use areas. Examples of constructed buffers might include green roofs inaccessible to humans or the positioning of quiet, lantern-like spaces (sleeping quarters) in zones – or ecotones – between human and nonhuman centered cores, with more active, noisy spaces located elsewhere.[18]

Compatibility between species needs and human constructs

Features designed to attract species can be biological traps if based on inadequate understanding of life cycle histories and if other stressors are not accounted for (for instance, the possibility of future development near the site or attractiveness of certain site features to predators, etc.). As an example of a comprehensive approach to urban morphology that acknowledges complex patterns of species behavior, a building feature such as a green roof may be configured to provide suitable habitat for birds. Meanwhile, nearby glazed façades that are faceted and otherwise highly visible would enable birds to detect their material presence, so strikes are less common.[19]

Critical need: health and population of species

When possible and viable, attempts should be made to conserve and/or create habitat for at-risk native plant and animal species. As environmental philosopher Bryan Norton argues, in most instances we lack extensive knowledge of the contribution of species to the overall ecosystem function. A prudent approach would be to assume a species has value and to work to ensure its mobility and long-term survival in a context where fragmentation prevails, as with Kephart who looks to the reserve potential of every available constructed surface.

Species expressive and formal qualities

In an approach best described as regionalist biomimicry, high-profile or "flagship" species with desired formal and behavioral qualities could inspire the design or architectural and configurations. The linchpin Oregon white oak, for example, has a pattern of growth and branching with distinctive shapeliness, structural integrity, and spatial complexity. Designers have an opportunity to translate experiential and functional characteristics of oaks into built forms to generate richly dynamic spatial settings.

As befits the complexity of this endeavor, the criteria prove inconsistent. For example, it may be desirable to attempt to support a sensitive species within a development given threats to survival, yet its status as threatened may be a function of lack of tolerance to noise, artificial light, etc., and its likelihood of colonization slim. This circumstance indicates how alterations to the urban fabric as strategic selections in natural history offer no substitute for conservation and rehabilitation of landscape-scale systems upon which a biologically diverse future depends. For many, consideration of target species in the design of site-scale urban redevelopment may be viewed as an act of desperate futility in an irrevocable context of mass extinction, paralleling captive breeding programs in zoos. Yet within this conscious and optimistic process of place-making lie great possibilities to bolster wildness latent in a world of multinaturals. Creatures colonize as they choose (or as the wind blows them), with numbers of examples in the city exceeding urban ecologists' wildest expectations. Motivated and knowledgeable teams equip themselves to fashion complex urban space as a furthering of biological opportunity.

Methodological evolutions and synergies

Development of a statement of goals and intentions for urban ecological design and management, matching habitat and development types, designing for species: these ways of operating underscore what Matthias Gross describes as a "the performance of inventing nature."[20] These preliminary efforts do not fix the problem rigidly, and "cooperation between different forms of knowledge production" continues through all phases of design, construction, and occupation.[21] Taken as a whole, a development undertaking is a reflective structuring of a dynamic community with correspondences to a model of ecology to which a group subscribes.

The ecologist Jeremy Jackson claims: "Ecosystem deterioration ... needs to be addressed by a series of bold experiments to test the success of integrated management."[22] With development sites as locations for regenerating natural communities, for recolonization, stopover, through passage, and other fulfillments of need, realized works of architecture become subjects and centers of adaptive (urban) ecosystem management, education, experimentation, and craft. Portions of projects declared free trade zones at boundaries of practice, for example the urban ecology-turned skyward investigations by the Center for Architecture Science and Ecology (CASE) corporate/academic partnership, become a form of relational aesthetics, "experimental niches that foster participation and learning to develop new ideas, new practices and knowledge."[23] While the frequency of change in societal values and priorities challenges research in the natural sciences that often requires prolonged observation, architectural sites of environmental knowledge can enable "higher frequency" hypothesis development that informs longer-term programs of study.

Natural scientists might rightfully scrutinize the lack of definitiveness of ecological goals articulated in association with a design undertaking and follow-up evaluations resting on (educated) assumptions about the reintroduction of core habitat, the desirability and size of buffer zones, the advantages for urban wildlife linkages, the impacts on certain species, etc. And yet it is the nature of a professional design inquiry to operate from incomplete premises and maximize learning opportunity in evaluating successes and shortcomings in the aftermath of construction. Given this trial-like capacity of the designer, and while recognizing that ecologists and architects perform a different calculus, attention to similarities between practices is warranted. Among ecologists, restorationists in particular shape environments by building consensus involving many agents while maintaining some creative control. Restoration ecologist Eric Higgs suggests: "The history of the field shows a plural practice, one reflecting the best of scientific perspicuity and creative tinkering."[24] He goes further: "Ecological restoration as a *design* discipline demands attention to tradition and novelty at the same time, searching across the spectrum of the arts and sciences for the best way to respect ecological and cultural integrity."[25] One could readily substitute "sustainable architecture" for "ecological restoration" in the previous sentence and, with the inclusion of landscape architecture as a critical mediating discipline, recognize what is at heart caring occupation of shared space and mutual ground.

Notes

1   Solomon 2003, 90.
2   Casey 1993, 259.
3   Gadamer 2004, 357.
4   From Paul Kephart's lecture at the April 2007 HOPES EcoDesign Conference.

5   See www.michaelsinger.com.

6   Gross 2003, 192.

7   Snyder 1990, 154.

8   This is a paraphrasing of a key point Fraser made during a lecture at the University of Oregon in 2006.

9   Koolhaas 1996, 336.

10 From a lecture Hester delivered at the HOPES EcoDesign Conference at the University of Oregon on April 6, 2013.

11 Rosenzweig 2003, 7.

12 McGinley 2008.

13 Cerra *et al.* 2008.

14 See Lundholm 2006.

15 Rosenzweig 2003, 78.

16 "Edge effect" refers to two adjacent and distinct landscape types/patches and their impact upon one another due to proximity.

17 Development often exacerbates the problems specialist species face by fragmenting and decreasing the area of cores and increasing their surface-to-volume ratio or rather the proportion of edge to core.

18 An ecotone refers to the transition area between two adjacent landscape patches; in some cases the area is small or narrow and the boundary distinct; in other cases, the transition area is more generous and threshold-like, where blending and "feathering" of the two patches occur.

19 Examples of bird friendly architectural design guides include: www. toronto.ca/lightsout/pdf/development_guidelines.pdf (Toronto), www. birdsandbuildings.org/info.html (Chicago), and; www.metrofieldguide. com/?page_id=530 (New York Audubon).

20 Gross 2003, 164.

21 Gross 2003, 175.

22 Jackson *et al.* 2001, 636.

23 CASE: www.case.rpi.edu/home.html; Relational aesthetics: see Bourriaud 2002; quote: Gross 2010, 176.

24 Higgs 2003, 82.

25 Higgs 2003, 279 (italics added).

CHAPTER 9

Assembling Context

She [art] makes and unmakes many worlds, and can draw the moon from heaven
with a scarlet thread.[1]

The architect surveys, gathers, and coalesces diverse contextual influences and
communicates these in complex graphic shorthand. Ecological considerations
enter this realm and invite change in perspective on relations between projects,
sites, and surroundings. Commissioned to design a project on a river or other
urban waterway, the ecologically conscious architect engages those involved in
its restoration and in keeping it at the forefront of public consciousness.
Subsequent design investigations build from this "riparianized" perspective,
foregrounding ecology in bearing witness to the life of urban waters. The river,
so critical in the history of many urbanized regions, yet so commonly hidden
from public view, acquires activating capacity and structuring presence as
opposed to a given worthy of contemplative appreciation from a perch on
the shore.

Poetic animation of a context's spatial structure and dynamism is fundamental
to architectural inquiry that moves beyond default assumptions of relationships
of use. Former student Paul Harman offered the idea of a "hollow within the
grid" as a condensed summary of a ten-acre site in southeast Portland, Oregon,
location of a proposed mixed-use development. Looking at an aerial image, the
"hollow" appears as a center, poised between neighborhoods, a highway, and
light rail stops and hugging a major urban creek. A section drawing and a hike
through brambles affirm a description of the site as a "hollow," a barely visible
sink and a gatherer of waters.

The question arises as to whether this ambivalent condition is positive or
negative. Does one engage a design and planning process motivated by concern

for overcoming the site's invisibility and expanding its presence? Or should the project reinforce the site's seclusion or otherwise work with its "hollowness"? Might a hollow-like site adjacent to a major urban creek collect and treat its own water and that of neighboring sites in a quiet, workman-like manner? Or is it a (conceptual) cut-and-fill operation where the designer elevates strategic portions of the site while maintaining a quiet posture for the remainder?

At this point, the role of architecture extends beyond that of solving a building program. In addition, the project is a reconfiguration of context, a reaffirmation of its key attributes and an activator within the trajectory of its ongoing constitution. Even in a context of rapid urbanization with no obvious nearby natural feature to re/uncover or immediate topographic presence to react to, a project team can nevertheless reintroduce traces of a natural history (or a hybrid of natures–cultures past) and harness assets of its setting (heat, light, wind, reflectance and other aspects of its constructed micro-ecological surroundings) in realizing a latent potential and in producing a newly intensified biome. Short of daylighting a creek, initial design investigations can claim and reclaim resources in reconditioning life.

The design team identifies a site's (multiple) roles and gives them names, apt and evocative descriptors capturing with particularity the activating qualities of context and the site's contribution relative to broader urban ecologies. Does a site serve to widen a green corridor or fill a gap to bring a corridor to fuller resolution? Is it an ecotone between distinct realms such as an upland forest, built outcrops, and an urban prairie? Is it a fortifying edge or a capacity-building center? Might it be a side channel, outgrowth, reservoir, conduit, ancillary pocket, extension, instigator, or stepping-stone?

Such descriptors can help enormously in generating impressions that register with collaborators and the client, and in the public eye. Creative articulations are acts of *assembling context*, construing meaning and instantiating a trajectory. Deleuze and Guattari attest: "One does not represent, one engenders and traverses."[2] Their biographer François Dosse maintains in turn: "Posing the right problem depends not on the ability to reveal what is but on the ability to invent."[3] That is to say, given the layered complexity of the site and limitless potential for interpretation, the story the designer tells reveals creative impetus as much as it discloses a truth of ecology. "Assembling context" makes explicit the necessity of projecting one's powers of observation outward, the riches to be found there, and the pre-given non-neutrality of what one seizes upon. Articulating the process of this assembling becomes a basis for meaningful action, an enactment of events that might occur in relation to a deeper recognition of one's own motivations.

Multiplicities

Aware of the importance of formulating environmental and design problems comprehensively, the diverse presences of a site and vicinity, habitat types and possible species to plan for, and the sway of one's conceptual predispositions, the design team is poised to generate initial organizational proposals for a project. The mediums the team employs ought to be numerous, accommodating a setting's complexity, fantastically imaginative, and communicative of both a clear set of intentions and the seeking of unforeseen possibility. Generation of multiple organizational iterations decreases individual ownership and intensifies dialog about priorities underlying a project, some pre-articulated, others emergent. When there is one proposal on the table, a designer may defend its validity as linked to her integrity: artifact and ego bond. When discussing a variety of possibilities, the ecology of merit, the focus shifts to the relative promise and perhaps consequences, whether intended or unforeseen, of formative moves. By testing a range of alternatives through expendable and cheap design experiments, designers gain confidence that hunches have value and see the advantages in alternatives. Quick deployments encourage willingness to reassign roles where functions attach to forms in manners that differ from those intended originally; the process avails itself to discovery, "role playing," evolutionary adaptation, and natural selection. Base drawings that fix or suspend certain conditions – blue horizontal lines in section indicating seasonally variable water levels of constructed wetlands – are underlays facilitating heightened awareness of and experimentation with spatial difference.

While architects often view building/landscape interactions as instigated by buildings and extending into the landscape, conditioning and transforming it in the process, value may be gained in a reversal (or perhaps ideally, a convergence, where larger contextual forces press inward and the amplitude of activity settings push outward, and the architectural environs becomes the considered, expressive resolution of these forces). As an inaugural design exploration, using aerials and topographic and other underlays, and with the site perhaps the size of a postage stamp and the context the size of a table (or their digital equivalents), the designer can identify larger-scale matrices of open spaces, tree canopy coverage, urban green structures, remnant water drainages, and the linkages between. Graphic investigations as inventive necessity enable the designer to study the repair or reinforcement of fabric and the ways green and blue (water) infrastructures become armatures around which a project evolves, grows, and adapts over time. *The building grows between the gardens.*

Graphic conventions have tremendous import; they have parallels to metaphors in language in that they are highly consequential and yet imperfect summations of a complex enterprise, privileging silently certain facets of this complexity over others. Latour and Yaneva see a disjunction between customary illustration and experience of architectural space: "Euclidean space is the space in which buildings are drawn on paper but not in which buildings are built – and even less the world in which they are lived."[4] A more explicitly ecological approach to architectural design calls for a choreography of overlapping "image types" at the intersection of spatial configuration, human experience, building behavior, and events and influences on a site and those that lie beyond. With this in mind, perhaps the conscious generation of graphic fragments, the intentional arrangement of comprehensive irresolution and collage-like associations of the dissimilar, is holistic, inclusive, and more "lived-in" in that the designer communicates potential between drawings and invites others to continue to share in what will be actualized. The punctured incompleteness of aerial site collages and perspectives in Witherford Watson Mann Architects' "Bankside Urban Forest" neighborhood plan proposal (a project as "landscape stitching," or the knotting of the diffuse and concentrated) provides an instance of this approach, very different from the many island-like, self-contained, "biospheric"

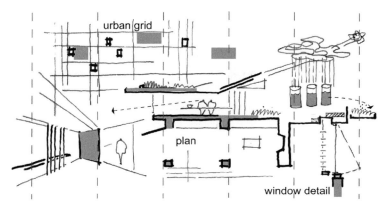

Graphic fragments as holistic irresolution in the conceptual stages of design, inviting connections between one another and the input of others.

images of proposals purported as visionary and green, vanishing point squarely in the middle of building masses.[5]

An appropriate ecology of graphic intervention, the construction of *arrays of image and words*, might involve graphic gaps, strategic disturbances, communities of line weights, dashes and dots. A "lived" manner of communicating built space suggests the desirability of drawings that converge or crystallize where functional, ecological elements and places of human activity coalesce. Conversely, these same representations can provide indications of elements with capacity and freedom to flow beyond or leap out of any one frame: water, wind, light.[6] Latour reminds us that even with smaller-scale, more circumscribed commissions:

> **We know perfectly well that we are not dealing with ordinary assemblies, with closed, concentrated spaces, but rather with flowing basins, as multiple as rivers, as dispersed as tributaries, as wild as the brooks on a map of France.[7]**

Continual unfolding and dispersal impel simultaneous representation of multiple time horizons: diurnal, seasonal, generational, geologic. Vincent James of VJAA in Minneapolis notes that much of the firm's design process focuses on "orchestrating and filtering temporal phenomena" and asserts, "architects need to think about the temporal field as much as they think about the form or appearance of the buildings themselves."[8] Given a goal to understand and communicate how architecture can support a larger biological reality, graphic depictions of movement, patterning, and life histories of species and flows and concentrations of energies and nutrients are productive forays in the realm of the temporal.

Von Uexkuell envisions and endeavors to describe "life worlds" of those other than humans: events that trigger nonhuman species' response, modes of inhabitation and migration, and the niches animals occupy in proximity to others.[9] A flight of imagination on the wing of a bat leads to graphic homing and wandering, mapping of resource networks, existing or potential, that could be augmented by project-scale development, and small detail sketches of immediate habitat structure. Section studies illuminate potential for multiple beings to occupy different strata within one vertical band of space, with trees growing alongside, up and over dwellings, providing summer shade for people below and corridor networks of limbs facilitating movement for creatures above. Watershed maps and models (historic and current) inform the tracing of a journey of a droplet of water from the cloudy sky through a site to the turbulent creek and facilitate careful recognition of a project as an event in support of biologically friendly urban hydrology. Rather than the customarily high level of resolution of a building and a ghosting of the landscape in an architectural proposition, or rendering of the landscape around a white blank-box building-as-placeholder in a landscape architectural investigation, stitching of relationships motivates graphic inquiry.

In playing out events and behaviors along a timeline, ecoarchitectural approaches to media ought to resonate with Latour's notion of the collective of humans and nonhumans ever expanding through inclusion of new entities or "propositions" and with Dempster's notion of ecosystems as adaptable, "sympoeitic" systems.[10] In this sense ecologically conscious architects employ the *media of possible events*. This dimension of multiplicity, the devising of open processes that invite diverse influence, suggests avoidance of excessive reliance on any one tool, however promising and seemingly comprehensive, and the value of moving between scales, image types, and work surfaces and stations. Chuck Eastman, champion of Building Information Modeling (BIM), predicts: "Eventually, the building model is expected to replace drawings, in the same way that the 'horseless carriage' eventually was replaced by the automobile."[11] Those who share this conviction may pay insufficient attention to an important facet of an empowering new tool for coordination, communication and figuration: the new means, by calling for replacement of standards, contains within it the seeds of its eventual displacement. This fits Deleuze and Guattari's framework of observation: what "reterritorializes" also, eventually, "deterritorializes"; what claims a space in order to operate opens that space to new, unforeseen operations that usher in eventual dislocation.[12]

Tools have purchase on habits, and the designer must create access points within a process to scrutinize critically assumptions underlying their use. In these revolutionary times digital tools allow rapid information feedback across platforms and modes of analysis, yet can also lead to higher levels of professional and disciplinary isolation. Architects fabricate digitally; landscape architects systematize geographic information. Innovation lies in formation of new chemical bonds in reaction to graphic and procedural atomization.

Often the simplest of tools offer tremendous leverage in fostering improvisation and pliancy in moving between looseness and precision, between informed and qualitative judgment, versus those more tightly choreographed, relentlessly repetitive and fortress-like in their impenetrability to outside influence. Rather than one tool as a motherboard, value resides in hybrid mediums that embrace the soul of the hand, the precision of the computer, the soul of the computer, and the precision of the flight pattern of a bird. Kaleidoscopic operations of graphic communication – including forms that are not proprietary – safeguard against closure.

Architectures of magical realism

A spirited design process parallels good fiction, is itself a form of storytelling where temporary suspension of reality creates a space of speculative truthfulness. Paul Ricoeur links fiction to potential reality in a manner akin to speculation about possible futures:

> Fiction addresses itself to deeply rooted potentialities of reality to the extent that they are absent from the actualities with which we deal in everyday life under the mode of empirical control and manipulation.[13]

A drawing created in the initial stages of a project investigation that communicates arrival at "the" solution does disservice to the project team as a learning community. A "fictive" graphic strategy, on the other hand, invites ambiguity, acknowledges truthfulness within a world of truths, and demonstrates commitment to a design process that reveals as it unfolds. A design approach as *drawing toward* active questions through open frames and dissimilar perspectives differs in kind from fixation around known models.

Oscar Wilde reminds us "truth is entirely and absolutely a matter of style."[14] With truth as style or manner of distinction, and expressive truthfulness in architectural design a transcription of context, a productive and creative process would involve speculative discrimination, for example removal of content to reveal nonphysical or otherwise distant proximities. The disappearance of the middle ground – Leatherbarrow's practical horizon – highlights potential linkages between individuals and groups and significant events and landscapes in the distance, between "equipmental" and "environmental" horizons. Valerie Gonzalez says of the Islamic architecture of Andalusia that one "draws a topography by juxtaposition of various isolated elements.[15] By intimating continuity, conscious omission lends significance to the remainder. This differs from (topo)graphic evenhandedness that may ultimately encourage the physical realization of sameness of weakly connected parts. Taking liberties in the sizes and shapes of drawings and the elements that comprise them allows such relational intensification despite remoteness, as with Smout Allen's diagram of technical performance in their Grand Egyptian Museum competition entry where the distant water source and the (ever) presence of water in the project are collapsed in one world.[16]

Oscar Wilde asserts: "Art is really a form of exaggeration; and selection, which is the very spirit of art, is nothing more than an intensified mode of over-emphasis."[17] To give weight to the delicate and to diffuse mass is to disclose potential truths that would remain hidden through more tepid undertakings. Mystery as inventive, graphic reassignment of location and roles abets imagination of worlds to be. As Robin Kirkpatrick celebrates in his introduction to his translation of Dante's *Paradiso*: "Mystery ceases to be the restrictive inhibition to inquiry that it has become since the Enlightenment and is revealed as the generative source of all active existence."[18] Mystery as a component to design may imply drawing and making tangible *invisible forces* that act on a site or on us (phenomena that one cannot see, but that have a presence nevertheless, like vapor or bedrock). Exaggeration, taking an investigation to the limits, puts in sharp relief the patterning and shaping power of that which eludes immediate impression in our everyday lives. It is like those who, by studying life at the extremes, contribute to understanding parameters of behavior in "normal" settings. According to Michael P. Cohen: "Because it is an edge, because it is sensitive to change, the timberline reveals the invisible flux of conditions that support lower-elevation terrestrial life, like humans."[19]

Although it may seem peculiar from the standpoint of sustainable architecture to take liberties in revealing properties inherent to materials and forces acting upon the world, graphic artifacts that embody ambiguity, dematerialization of the massive, and registration of the ineffable signal the kind of tissue that might connect across myriad dimensions of environmental challenge. By disclosing its fabrication in an attempt to understand and approximate the real, a drawing can engender awareness of both the social construction and the pressing realness of ecological circumstances. There is value in that. In figuring out how things might work and delight at the same time, designers summon schemes with the insightfulness of a poet or artist who appreciates the contribution of science. According to Donald Schoen:

In the terrain of professional practice, applied science and research-based technique occupy a critically important though limited territory, bounded on several sides by artistry. There are an art of problem framing, an art of implementation, and an art of improvisation – all necessary to mediate the use in practice of applied science and technique.[20]

Arts that inhere in ecological architectural design are directed toward the promise of grounding the fantastical in the terrain we occupy. The gardens of Villa d'Este in Tivoli are an astonishing example of the finite turned infinite, an elaboration of aqueous reality as designed exuberance, transference and shifting of states as commentary on continuity. The gardens honor the many presences of water, acknowledging while making light of the rules governing it, musing on the forces of gravity, and drawing people to its many features in ways that cause wonderment and thermal delight. Today, a more consciously artistic and democratic ecological approach to design might employ frivolity as a strategy of efficiency and celebrate the scenography of a multitude of beings in everyday urban environments. There is theatrical potential to the ecological design of the city, a staging of nature heightening perception of unending sequences of props that exist beyond and beside the spectacle at hand. Ecologically architectural graphics script the performance of an urban nature.

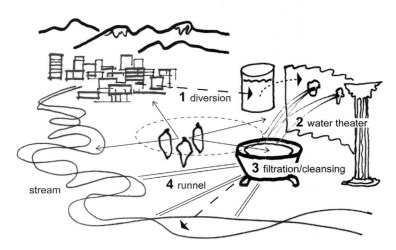

Theatricality in the making of ecological performance.

Notes

1   Wilde 1969, 306.
2   Deleuze and Guattari 1987, 364.
3   Dosse 2010, 140.
4   Latour and Yaneva 2008, 80.
5   See Littlefield 2012, 44.
6   Steven Holl's isometric drawing of the Stretto House for instance depicts the structuring capacity of water. See Holl *et al*. 1994, 146.
7   Latour 2004, 165.
8   James and Yoos 2006, 67.
9   See Von Uexküll 1957. "Life worlds" is the primary theme of Von Uexküll's essay.
10 See Latour 2004 for a description of human/nonhuman propositions and Dempster 2007 for a description of sympoeitic systems.
11 Eastman 2009, 16.
12 Architect and theorist Teddy Cruz offers captivating parallel observations of processes of deterritorializing and reterritorializing with respect to redevelopment projects in downtowns of major American cities: for every "megaproject" there are innumerable, poorly represented, and very real marginalization projects that will, through their cumulative mass, eventually force their attentions upon us.
13 Ricoeur 1978, 152–153.
14 Wilde 1969, 305.
15 Gonzalez 2001, 109.
16 See Smout Allen 2007.
17 Wilde 1969, 302.
18 Kirkpatrick 2003, xivi.
19 Cohen 1998, 114.
20 Schoen 1987, 13.

CHAPTER 10

Continuity of Singularities

Between nature and man form intervenes.[1]

Designers employ ordering systems as a means of achieving spatial clarity and richness of organization while contending with the complexities that characterize design endeavors. Order is architectural grammar, the rhythmic patterning of space, and a play of resemblance and dissimilarity.

Marsilio Ficino's writings offer a window to ideas of order during the Renaissance, with the pyramid providing a clear figure for the relationships obtaining between species, humans, and God, and where architecture serves as harmonization of hierarchical stratification emanating from above and based on gradients of value. What does a bridging of architectures and natures suggest today as far as notions of order and the meaning of figures of representation? To what extent does unity of expression hold sway, in which elements are stitched together within a more encompassing armature? How might the designer interested in these relationships acknowledge the dizzyingly intricate nature of ecosystems as described by ecologists such as Henry Gleason, where graded differences exist and where fine degrees of connection and disconnection characterize organic–inorganic assemblages?[2] If organizations of architecture have been informed historically by convictions of the patterning of natural orders, what are the design implications of greater historical awareness of the provisional nature of constructions of order?

If the spatiality of symbolization of bodies and nature remains a relevant architectural striving, and if it becomes increasingly ineffectual to isolate a building as a subject of aesthetic contemplation, the distribution of attributes residing within orders will evolve. Paul Kephart's concern for "how to show ecological vernacular" invites more lateralized aesthetic transpiration.[3]

If, according to Richard Dawkins, "individuals are temporary meeting points on the crisscrossing routes that genes take through history,"[4] rather than reconciling multiplicity into unity (as the Neoplatonist Marsilio Ficino would recommend), one postmodern emphasis for designers concerned with relational expression might be that of multiplying unions, that is, establishing accessible systems of transaction for open ecological operations.

The cadence, manner, and congruity of ecoarchitectural orders depend greatly on the nature of the project and the character of the site and setting. One expressive tendency multiplies unions and intensifies awareness of the other by distinguishing realms sharply. As ecologist collaborators might recommend, portions of the site should be made inaccessible to people in order to protect sensitive and threatened species. Negotiations over the space necessary to permit base level function and the desired segregation of human and natural territory prevail in scientific and regulatory discourse, for example in environmental protection legislation, planning bylaws, codes, research recommendations, etc. ("structures are not permitted within 100 feet of the stream embankment"). These distinctions also ground expression in numerous and celebrated endeavors in historic and contemporary art and architecture, for example the abstractly "white" and orthogonal residential projects of the New York Five architects in the 1970s, standing in sharp contrast to surrounding fields and woods.[5]

As one example of intensified co-presence, building wings and façades might operate as theater sets, backdrops setting off singular landscape architectural elements such as a raingardens and events they make possible, for instance brief encounters between people on lunch breaks and birds attracted to these rest areas during migrations. Architectural elements can cohere as a datum, frame, or series of planes that, through their stable configuration, elevate awareness of both the cyclical temporality and the sudden emergence of landscape and ecological "happenings." Conversely, landscape (ecological) features might frame the theater of life taking place within human focused interiors.

Architectural framing devices can increase the didactic value and experimental potential of an urban ecological landscape. A bracketed space encourages

Architecture as horizon with frames binding sky and earth.

measurement and counting, analysis of effects of orientation, changes of occupation and intensity, attractiveness of features to colonization, etc. A framed landscape space is a real-time, life-size, three-dimensional graph facilitating plotting and comparison.

Architectural and ecological identities might engage at one critical spatial, aesthetic, and functional ecotone, an overlap zone of demarcated realms where select entities extend tendril-like, one into the other. A rest area commons breaks out of a building mass and merges into a life-worldly garden, a habitat patch extends to and fills the void of a building mass, the ellipse of a drainage meadow punctuates and animates an unconditioned hallway, a living screen branches into a vertical circulation spine: select and spatially charged tissues connect distinct architectural and landscape ecological rooms (symbolic or otherwise). These overlap zones can heighten occupants' connections to ambient conditions and provide basic levels of environmental comfort while acting as outlets, stopovers, and identity markers for those – humans and others – making their way through the commons, campus, and city.

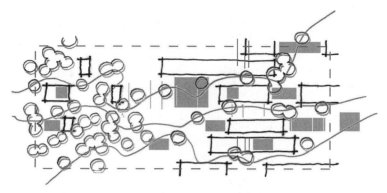

Builtscapes and landscapes intermingle, tendril-like.

In considering advantages of projects with distinct yet mutually reinforcing zones of space and with selected areas of overlap, the scale of investigation becomes critically important. If at the site both architectural and ecological elements are incorporated yet largely demarcated, and if numerous projects in an urban district are organized along similar lines, an aerial vantage would reveal a level of neighborhood integration between landscape, ecological, and built systems perhaps never before achieved in the city!

Plurality of opposed continuousness

> Native American maps did not rely on fixed points within a bounded space but on patterns of intersected lines.[6]

The environmental philosopher David Wood deploys the metaphor of the Möbius strip as an indicator of reciprocity of order between humans and nature in that it allows

> for the idea that radical opposition can be combined with deep ontological continuity: at every point two sides but one surface. This gives us a beautiful way of representing man's relation to nature – opposed, in some sense, and yet at the same time continuous.[7]

A beautiful representation indeed, and yet is it not emblematic of the constraints of a dualistic model, positioning humans too singularly as/on the other side of nature? With the German biologist Jacob Johann Von Uexküll's diverse "phenomenal self-worlds" in mind, might there not be numerous (countless) Möbius strips, with newt on the one side, nature on the other, Chinook on one side, nature on another, newt on one side, Chinook on the other?[8] Multiplicity as both species diversity and diversity within species would seem to implode the concept of *opposed* continuousness.

A fine-grained, ecologically inspired ordering operation, one that accounts for a plurality of self-worlds and translates across particularities of built and natural, would involve collage-like superimpositions of quasi-autonomous sets or subsets: a set of understory communities, a subset of paths, a building façade subset, etc. Increments are fine and numerous, harlequin. Each set is identifiable as such, and is made of elements that operate *consistently* relative to other elements that make up the set (this is not to say elements in sets are identical to one another, only to say they share common properties and roles). Sets are related to one another in an *inconsistent* manner, as their character and dynamics differ; this leads to a "play of juxtapositions" between elements

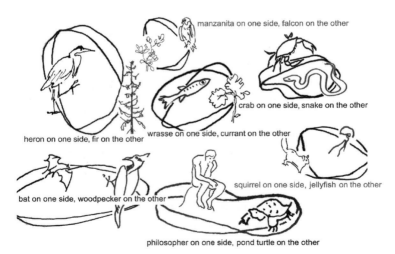

An endless array of Mobius strips?

corresponding to different sets. The patterning of the whole leads to perception of **individual elements assuming singularity** despite belonging to a set, precisely because of the uniqueness of relations with individuals of other sets in comparison to those of their own set. As an aggregate, it is not simply that "richness exists in the experience of subsets" but that it exists in the experience of richly interwoven coincidences of – and functional interplays between – constellations of elements across sets.[9]

Such an approach to order, celebrating the presence of individuals while situating them in a distinctive collective, contributes to our sense of a **continuity of singularities**. As Gilles Deleuze envisions: "Although they are not continuous, singularities belong fully to continuousness."[10] Though simultaneous breaks and connections are of a different nature than the plasticity of the baroque, manners of convergence exist nevertheless, as Deleuze's theoretical explorations on baroque sensibility suggest: "The really distinct is neither necessarily separate nor separable, and the inseparable can be really distinct."[11] Together, Deleuze and Guattari address explicitly the otherness of subsets and the polyphony of the ecological ensemble:

> **Every territory encompasses or cuts across the territories of other species, or intercepts the trajectory of animals without territories, forming interspecies junction points. It is in this sense that, to start with, Von Uexkuell develops a melodic, polyphonic, and contrapuntal conception of nature.[12]**

This outlook admits both/and conditions of ambiguous clarity where the nature of one system (the façade of a building, for example) is celebrated as distinct from the nature of another (an upland prairie garden, for example), and yet where the two (and many more) orders can coexist, engage selectively, and thrive. In some instances members of different sets come into physical contact and provide mutual support. Conversely, elements of the same set may never touch, but there is connectivity and continuity all the same, as with the branching of oaks or the spacing of columns. What is important is that relationships between elements constituting different sets produce spatial and functional asymmetries. Some systems stretch and scatter, others clump or

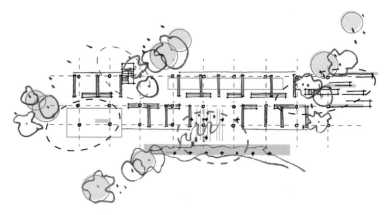

"A shimmering through of varying density": elements cohere as sets yet maintain inconsistent relationships with elements comprising other sets.

swarm. Sets operate at different frequencies and form vortices and disturbances when they meet. Their various trajectories generate a multiplicity of spatial conditions, read as a continuum of localized patterns, like "speed approaching that of alternating current, so that alternation is sensed as a single continuous perception."[13]

A great advantage of "continuity of singularities" is a welcoming of those inevitable "factors that are as yet unknown" described by Günter Behnisch.[14] Far into a design project the client, fire marshal, or planning authority asks that a new condition be satisfied; the designer willingly incorporates this request as a new compositional "layer," in contrast to a purer aesthetic where the unanticipated undermines the system. For Behnisch and Partners, this situationalism of process and order is representative of a diverse, inclusive, and pluralistic German society, standing out optimistically against the somber uniformity and imposing monumentality that epitomized darker times in the nation's history. Sets often cohere as pure geometries, for example column grids (especially column grids given the structural engineer's desire to predict behavior in distributing and carrying loads); sets can also be relatively free. The classrooms of Behnisch's Saint Benno School in Dresden are, given budget and function, highly rational, rectangular volumes: light-filled, gem-like boxes. And yet the boxes are arranged informally relative to one another – they do not cohere into a grid-like pattern and instead "dance." The residual hallway space that forms between the classrooms and the blue multi-story wall that shelters the school from the busy adjacent street takes on a landscape-like character; it widens and narrows by virtue of deployment of classroom boxes, admits natural light from unexpected sources, and opens to sudden, oblique views of a protected garden. As typical in Behnisch and Partners' work, even color lifts itself from a field to form new sets and affiliations and liberate others in the process.

These "loose" yet rigorous ordering systems, the exploratory, animated forms and fingerlike extensions, what Behnisch architect Christian Kandzia describes as "a shimmering through of varying density," anticipate a more encompassing approach that includes sets emanating from the landscape.[15] As these are pursued and represented, rather than assuming as with environmental philosopher Allen Carlson that "the natural environment … has a certain openness and indeterminateness that makes it an unlikely place to find formal qualities," designers can utilize this very indeterminateness as a basis for the formal qualities most desired, a fragmentary aesthetics of elements collaged from the multiplicity.[16] Instead of interconnections amongst discrete elements in closed systems, the emphasis shifts to momentary singularity of non-discrete elements in open systems, momentum of connectivity leading to disconnection, and stability harboring tensions of subsequent unrest.

Utilizing this approach to order and working with ecologists, designers can hypothesize as to what dynamics might be encouraged in a particular setting through introduction of supportive and open-ended organizational structures. In so doing, designers are alerted to the inherent incompleteness of architectural undertakings, thereby relieving some of the load – psychic, material, and thermodynamic – they have assumed building projects must carry. Such structures, both planned and provisional, offer aesthetic resonance as they give way, become obscured, or undergo metamorphosis as plant and animal communities find purchase. As Johnson and Hill suggest: "A second generative metaphor we consider useful in linking design and ecology is that of a scaffold as a structure that allows new forms to be constructed but does not determine those forms completely."[17]

Weak *and* robust, emulative *and* supportive architectures operate as "incommensurable elements in a disjunctive synthesis," connecting our migratory proto-urbanisms with those of other species.[18]

Fine grained de-centering

Fine-grained ordering operations, an approach that might also be described as rhythmic interspersing and nesting, involve extremes of interdigitation between built and natural realms resulting from continual folding and an increase in the number of elements contained within any one fold. The building is not the primary focus, and there are innumerable vanishing points. Ecological vectors perform a doubling back, puncturing, stippling, and activating architectural skins while pressing inward, reassembling interiors and finally reprojecting function and contour out to the garden. The designer first disentangles and consciously recombines elements within micro-systems. Tight ecoarchitectural

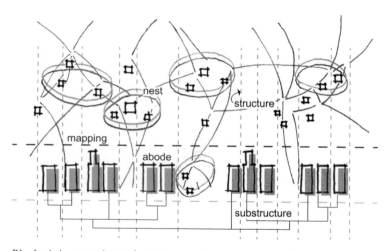

Rhythmic interspersing and nesting: complex space made of simple non-hierarchical elements that facilitate movement and connectivity.

choreography does not mean that every constructed element reinforces a hierarchy; rather less formally strict arrays of paths, platforms, and entry points are directed toward the attraction and pooling elements of diverse identity and purpose. Less constricted architectural orders enable formation of allegiances of others and foreground the preciousness of events. The ecological as material for the city is tracery of the innumerable, directed and spontaneous, that enlivens everyday urban affairs.

Architectural ecologies become rate-structured hierarchies, pixellations, pockets and knots of alternating, interchanging systems. Matrices of biological communities expand upon trellis buildings. Fields of light-filtering rooftop hedgerows hover above columnar grafts. Arrays of nest boxes shade and enliven rainscreen façades that are themselves purchases for cavity nesters and micro-entrapments of air, moisture, heat, and light: elements in diverse combination and quick succession. Path streams provide walking surfaces while acting as micro-hydrological channels and cleansers. Mosaics of colored surfaces attract pollinators to adjacent, interstitial gardens so that architectures become explicit components in the melodic refrains and couplings of the organic and inorganic.

Shannon McGinley recognizes: "Architects deal with the same basic elements as ecology: composition, structure and function."[19] Given these parallels, the designer is free to reconstitute architectural and ecological identities and anticipate that byproducts of any one system will continue to animate and transform others over time. The philosopher Bryan Norton suggests: "From quantum physics to ecological theory the epistemological lesson is the same: each action, even if it is a measuring action, changes the system in which it intervenes."[20] Art historian Henri Focillon would revel in a simultaneous reversal and preservation of identity and announcement of each in the other: "This delightful emulation and this interest in transpositions – which seeks the artificial at the heart of nature and the secret labor of nature at the heart of human invention."[21]

Newly introduced ecological infrastructures can build upon existing orders and patterns of use. The urban grid as matrix of endless extension of economic opportunity, in many ways the great neutralizer of (natural) otherness, might provide the framework for ecologically inclusive, spatially heterogeneous systems. To "butterfly" or "pixelate" the block is a means to preserve the grid's lineaments while establishing new experimental grounds and testing of beds, to facilitate gap formation and other processes of diversification and reclamation. Superimposition of new layers (stormwater alleys and pollinator corridors) inspired by and that fortify biological and hydrological processes augment the functional capacity of the inherited order of streets. The latter preserve block-like formality while inner courts perform a different, more fluid manner of work and assume less fixed identities in the process. A green corridor introduced on a site, swaths of trees and understory vegetation that facilitate wildlife movement and links to larger urban ecological networks, or a pool that collects and retains water: these create "openings" that might positively establish more airy, animated block interiors and buildings that in turn benefit from the presence of life.

Whatever the organizational approach, an overall goal would be to expand the palette of "eco-revelatory" design, a movement in the field of landscape architecture that endeavors to make visible and express ecological processes. The authors of the introduction to a special issue of *Landscape Journal* devoted to eco-revelatory design suggest: "By variously highlighting the particular ecological relationships at any given site, such design can punctuate and enliven our environment and sensitize us to what is known about its interlocking complexities."[22] While ecological systems are interrelated and complex, with

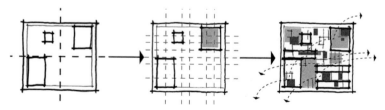

Pixelate the block: superimposition of a spatial structure in the cause of biological heterogeneity and experimentation (derived from David Wong's Master of Architecture comprehensive (thesis) design studio project, 2013).

many species' interactions with their life-worlds exhibiting a dovetailing or interlocking quality, for many others the patterning is more open-ended and less consistently enmeshed. Most critically, of concern is both the highlighting of ecological processes *and* the expression of the manner of revealing, the aesthetics of human comportment and sensitive commitment in affecting these processes.

With every work a pattern of intention, architectural ordering systems have potential to impact, express, and instigate natural systems processes, respond to habitat needs and life cycles histories, and encourage opportunities for awareness, learning, and experimentation.[23] The life cycle of the endangered western pond turtle, not typically a concern of the architect (unless legal action is being taken), can prompt formation of a spatio-temporal set, increasing both viability of the species and richness of the transcript of architectural orders. Patterning of order as selective drawing back and intensified mutual engagement invites initiative in excess of the fully planned and controlled, enables thinking along the lines of birds and mountains, and leads to the possibility of giving "birth to new modes of existence, closer to animals and rocks."[24]

Notes

1 Focillon 1992, 124.
2 For a consideration of Gleason's scientific and philosophical views of ecosystems and ecology, see Barbour 1996.
3 Personal correspondence with Paul Kephart, January 2008.
4 Dawkins 2004, 61.
5 The New York Five: Peter Eisenman, Michael Graves, Charles Gwathmey, John Hejduk, and Richard Meier.
6 Calloway 2003, 11.
7 Wood 2005, 44.
8 See Von Uexküll 1957.
9 Treib 1979, 32.
10 Deleuze 1993, 20.
11 Deleuze 1993, 55–56.

12 Deleuze and Guattari, 1994, 185. Perhaps this represents a baroque sensibility after all. As Christian Kandzia said of the design of Behnisch & Partners' Eichstatt Library – a project inspired by the notion of continuity of singularities – a goal was that of "breaking up solid forms with illusory devices" (from his lecture at the University of Oregon, October 21, 2011).

13 Treib 1979, 37.

14 From the transcript of a lecture that Guenther Behnisch delivered at the University of Oregon School of Architecture and Allied Arts, May 1990.

15 The quote comes from Christian Kandzia's lecture at the University of Oregon, October 21, 2011. Along a similar line of thought, Valerie Gonzalez (2001, 53) describes this as a "prism of artistic wonderment."

16 Carlson 2000, 37.

17 Johnson and Hill 2002, 15.

18 Dosse 2010, 153.

19 McGinley 2008.

20 Norton 1987, 205.

21 Focillon 1992, 98.

22 Brown *et al.* 1998, x.

23 See Baxandall 1985 for a detailed consideration of the way a creative work may be understood as a pattern of intention.

24 Deleuze and Guattari 1994, 74–75.

CHAPTER 11

Watermark

Poised amidst bodies of water in the city subject to cumulative impacts of nonpoint source pollution, architectures can go to work absorbing, conveying, and distributing stormwater and in so doing influence the survival probabilities of numerous species.[1] Site-scale projects can operate as "set pieces" structuring the movement of water; these works can do more than shed and become active components of watersheds. If Low-Impact Development (LID) offers a preferred and more sustainable alternative to impervious urban landscapes, a high-impact approach promises a friction-inducing architectural morphology that adapts to pulses, transforms flows, and captures and releases in dynamic response to biological need.[2] Opportunities for space-making, celebrating and symbolizing water as life source are numerous. An aqueous architecture fulfills the hopes of Katherine Rinne, expert on water infrastructure in Renaissance Rome, that whatever water's manner, shape, and journey, "it deserves to be revealed, honored and articulated."[3]

As discussed in chapter 8, the presence and abundance of certain species provide indications of the condition of larger ecosystems and the effects of urbanization, climate change, and other human-influenced factors. For instance, healthy wild salmon populations in the Pacific Northwest offer evidence of regional watershed and riparian habitat quality and the state of forest ecosystems.[4] The research of Nat Scholz and his collaborators at the National Oceanic and Atmospheric Administration (NOAA) demonstrates the toxic effects of nonpoint source pollutants on coho salmon moving upstream through urban waterways – one example of a species negotiating the perils of the city with limited success. In response to this and a growing body of research overall, regulatory agencies, nonprofits, and activists in the region are encouraging adoption of integrated stormwater practices with the hope that greater numbers of salmon, so central to the cultural landscape and identity of the region, can make their way to upper reaches of rivers and spawn. Future prospects for "salmon in the city" will depend in part on what becomes of water on an elaborated journey from rainclouds to urban sites, through and across roadways, buildings, and other urban elements and into waterways.[5] A democratization of amelioration of impact, a broad-based overhaul of everyday urban landscapes, is but one platform necessary for coho to survive.

To see the potential of a site-scale architectural intervention as constructive participant in the watershed is to account for and reconcile pre-development habitat conditions, shrinking storage and absorption capacities of urban landscapes, the spatially constrained realities of the growing city, and the likelihood of weather events of greater severity in a context of climate change. This combination of factors indicates the need for landscape-scale mitigation reserves that can accommodate stormwater, as well as intelligent appropriation of patches and pockets within the urban matrix. Imagining the participation of an architectural project as water-collector patch begins by situating it within its topographic, geological, and urban setting, placing it in relation to nearby structures and bodies of water, and considering how other attributes of the design problem, building program, and envelope, for example, can be enlisted and tested in shaping a new course.

A work of architecture as an aqueous sponge or an assemblage of micro-purifying rivulets could collect, decelerate, and filter water during peak rain events and deliver cleaner, cooler water to urban streams and wetlands at a cadence that helps keep channelized bodies from overflowing. A project could function as a threshold-like juncture, an oxygenating rift, where water flows act as dramatic tissue linking distinct bodies and define planes of activity in symbolic axial alignment with prominent environmental features – sources and sinks – at a remove. A project could be conceptualized as strategic placement of stone-like masses that form eddies of stepped pools that stage processes of filtration. Building volumes could frame and open to bodies that reflect the starry firmament while recharging the ground: the cosmology of pools, skylight, and dusky ultramarine ceiling of Williams and Tsien's Cranbrook Academy

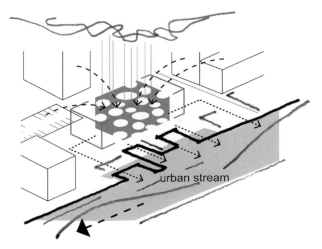

urban stream

A work of architecture as an aqueous sponge.

Natatorium turns outward and undergoes spatial pressurization by densely limitless atmospheres above and below.

Planes, conduits, pools, vessels, micro-rivulets, sponges, stepping-stones, sheets: these elements, at the same time as they contribute to a greater ecological good, can act as indices of the passage of time, reflective animators of a broader reality, and collectors and expanding outlets of constricted urban space. Rain garden courts can mirror the migrations of geese and sudden bursts of wind. Integrated storage batteries might declare arrival on site while alluding to the historical subsurface hydrology of the district. Movement and filtration of water from building to landscape can guide the journey of passersby: people and water can flow in parallel or conversely follow opposing paths that overlap and collect in spaces of charged occasion.

Architectures accommodating and instigating dynamic forces

Restoration ecologist Eric Higgs inquires as to the nature of a human intervention "that privileges unpredictable ecological processes."[6] Higgs' speculation is an inducement for the designer to consider more profoundly how the dynamism of weather events such as rainstorms and the registration of their intensity might have a formative influence over the physical configuration of materials. Numerous routes of flow from building to urban landscape could be established, in scuppers, along and through channels, and between pools, with the severity of the event dictating the path. An ordered multiplicity of watercourses and a linked diversity of collectors might better connect city-dwellers to the temperament and power of the indeterminate, fluctuating landscapes in which they are immersed.

Taking a cue from Kenneth Frampton, a "place-form" component of a work of architecture, made of earthen materials such as concrete and stone, would shape and negotiate water and ground. Patinas on these materials created by water could mark longer-term patterns of duration and intensity. The place-form would operate in expressive contrast to a "product-form," a more rational assembly of "overlapping, redundant surfaces" of higher-tech materials that would filter and shed while hovering above a site.[7] The conversation between the two forms in association with the dynamism of water generates a new perception of utility and occupation in an urban setting customarily appreciated for a high level of environmental predictability.[8]

A riverfront development offers a special instance of architecture as expressive structuring of mixture and separation, of built form as transmission between rain, run-off, and waterways and between humans drawn to water and conditions necessary for riparian habitat function. Architectural elements and stormwater retention features held at a physical remove from banks of waterways to ensure sufficient buffer and the space necessary to filter pollutants can nevertheless serve to celebrate the inauguration and destination of rainwater, structure views of the watershed, and otherwise foster association. Occupying the spaces between collection and conveyance, and between suspended water on a roof or in a raingarden and a nearby body that will eventually convey it, people are afforded a heightened impression of the dynamics of landscape.

Beechie and Bolton argue that in attempts to improve riparian conditions, a primary focus should be on "restoring and managing watershed processes rather than individual habitat characteristics," as well as "diagnosing and treating causes of habitat degradation rather than effects of habitat degradation."[9] In contending with a site on or near a severely degraded urban creek, perhaps one that is buried, designer/ecologist teams might experiment with dechannelization, riparian corridor expansion, and side channel creation as formative to combined processes of site restoration and development. ("Dechannelization" refers to the reworking of the shape/profile of a water body such as a stream or river, enabling a depressurization through widening that allows the body to assume biological and aquatic functions more in keeping with its prechannelized state. Dechannelization can be a form of rewilding urban landscapes, perhaps paradoxically as a function of urban redevelopment.) In an ordering operation akin to "rhythmic interspersing and nesting" discussed previously, placement of new buildings could help frame and form side channels that in turn serve as *refugia*, safe havens for aquatic species such as small fish to retreat to during major rain events and increased flow. Built forms as participants in a larger palette of sensitive intervention might help to hold back, filter, direct, and oxygenate water, provide coolth and shade, and serve as an armature for the recruitment of vegetation. In urban contexts that concentrate economic and environmental pressures, architectures might interact with, and quite possibly instigate and offer an outlet for, processes that are fluid and dynamic.

Architecture as prosthetic

Projects at a physical remove from water bodies can build on a narrative of association between processes of cleansing water and the state of a regional system and make an ecological contribution in ways seemingly disproportionate to their size. In their speculative "Center for the Life of Urban Waters," Andi Solk and Jeff Vincent propose a highly poetic bio-hydrological "machine" for a piazza in the densely settled historical center of Rome. Upon entering the piazza from any one of the adjacent alleys, one descends a broad ramp into a subterranean space organized around a pool of clear still water (the journey of the people and the water are reversed, and one is first greeted with water that has already percolated through the machine). One then ascends a stair through a narrow slot shaped by tall stacks of concrete block-like forms that hold sand and filter and cleanse water collected from nearby rooftops. Arriving on the horizontal plane of roofs of neighboring buildings, one is greeted by vibrant blossoms and aromas of numerous gardens in the foreground, the ubiquitous roof gardens of Rome, as well as views of aqueducts and "head" fountains in the distance (head fountains serve as the termini of aqueducts and present a "face" to the water as it is introduced to the city). Finally, one descends a filigree stair through matrix-like screens of "trays" of aromatic plants that filter graywater from nearby apartments and sunlight from above.

A modest proposal that could be replicated throughout public spaces in the city collapses architecture and ecology as well as scale and distance, linking the immediacy of tactile experience (the coolth of the stairwell between water-saturated blocks of sand), the pulse of a neighborhood, and visual ties to a regional hydrological context. An ecological architecture is synchronization of everyday perception and landscape-scale events, in this case involving an epic narrative of water and civilization. "Stacking value" pertains to the

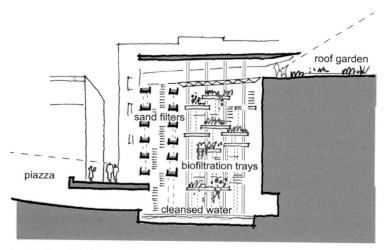

Andi Solk and Jeff Vincent's proposal for an "eco-architectural machine": architecture as elaboration of the urban journey of storm and graywater.

establishment of localized assemblages that align heightened multi-sensory awareness, sociability, and expressive performance. In this dense urban setting, a bio-hydrological architectural machine binds the elegant, urbane, and classically proportioned, the city as garden, neighboring buildings, ongoing educational demonstration, filigrees of texture, green shadows, and cooling purification. Working from a hierarchy notion of ecosystems, intervention in the aquatic system serves as a stabilizing event causing favorable constraints in subsequent behavior. In a city with a water supply of tremendously high quality and a polluted, underappreciated river, the Center is a device of augmentation and a move in an urban game inviting the next play.

Architectures of adaptive response

As an extreme example that responds to the landscape architect Randoph Hester's call to go straight to the source of conflict, design teams might link more explicitly the behavior of environmentally problematic buildings (parking garages as one particularly challenging example) to specific biological needs and constraints associated with urban waterways.[10] An exercise in linguistic activism might help at the outset: labeling a place to park a "garage" or "lot" increases the likelihood of an outcome that is conventional, dimly lit, and uninspiring. Following the landscape architect Walter Hood's advice to "remain quieter for awhile," and acknowledging limitations of the "idea of a type as a very closed thing," other descriptors might find their way into parlance: parking "gardens," parking "orchards," "marshes," "automobile forest filtration stations," or "perched biological threshold machines."[11] Metaphors begin a process of creative disturbance allowing for humanization of urban space in combination with enhanced environmental capacity.

Parking garages are stacked trays built for the purpose of storing idle automobiles, an expensive use of urban rooms and landscapes. Yet a benefit is that garages sequester cars temporarily. It is conceivable therefore that parking structures could "harvest" the particulates and pollutants cars generate that degrade water quality and aquatic habitat dramatically. By concentrating the problem, the impact may be ameliorated. Rainwater falling on the top level of a parking garage and on neighboring buildings could be directed along parking surfaces and collected in cisterns integral to the garage's design. It would be removed from the urbanized hydrological cycle so that cleansing structures such as hanging raingardens and bioswales could go to work to treat this water. This treated water would be released in turn to urban streams in a pulse-like manner analogous, but not identical to, the historical dynamism of the hydrological system.

As with the Center for the Life of Urban Waters, a parking wetland functions as an intervention in a context of lethal toxicity, with delivery to water bodies timed in a manner friendly to native aquatic species (fish moving upstream would benefit from a greater abundance of relatively cool and clean water delivered by the garage filter). A parking garage as an ecoarchitectural machine becomes a hydrological "speed bump," one among many in the coursings of water in the city. It belongs to a partner network of intelligent structures responding and adapting in real time to biological need.

Whatever the role and position of a project in the watershed, in stacking value and reconciling human needs and natural systems function, the designer plays

1 sensor linking intelligent building to stream detects cue (movement, temperature, other)

2 building shares information with others

3 ensemble of buildings reacts (releases treated water, other)

Biological cues in the urban landscape trigger a work of architecture to act with others in providing timely, beneficial response.

with increasing surface area. Deleuze's notion of the fold, a surface doubling back continually, acquires renewed architectural significance when considering the movement of water in urban landscapes. Stretching and contortion of paths enable a slowing down of rates of flow, the suspension and deposition of particulates, and increased spatial and habitat diversity. The forested landscape, elaborating as it does the passage of water from misty clouds to the gray-black roils of the creek, offers a model for envisioning undulating built urban forests. The prattle of drops collects on foliage and streams along darkening fissures of bark. Decaying matter littering the forest floor absorbs this surcharge, sponge-like. A designed proliferation of surfaces and features could emulate this performance and at a range of scales, from micro-channels as part of the outer layer of rainscreen-type building façades, to filtered terraces and conduits structuring site development, to collecting mediums articulating linkages between sites.

Reassessment of the value of underutilized space and the desirability of prolonged transference prompt metaphorical constructs emphasizing surface tension, hovering over and passing through, the staggering of eddies and the incorporation of relief valves, variegation, scored, raked, and mottled surfaces, increase in roughness coefficient, and offsets in the x, y, and z. A challenge becomes that of achieving "efficient inefficiencies," where certain elements retain compact shapeliness, formal simplicity, and high surface-to-volume ratios (thermal envelopes of buildings, for example), while associated features gain in morphological complexity in support of hydrological and habitat function, and where advantage is sought in the interstices. Biomimicry of a hydro-architectural nature is one of intricate abundance and thrift.

"Watermark" furnishes appropriately indeterminate imagery to conclude this chapter and draw connections to earlier discussions of design in relation to nature, the body, and metaphor.[12] Maurice Merleau-Ponty's writings on the organism as "watermark" convey impressions of fragility and semi-visibility, delicacy rather than overbearing expression, traces of making and residue of activity recorded in the negative and the hollowed. Embossing of fields leads to gossamer interactions of materiality and light; infusion of water patterns space.

Recognizing the impossibility of speaking of a watermark without mindfulness of the surface on which it is impressed, perhaps one ought not speak of a project without consideration of the textures and profiles underlying it, the presences and pressures that are part of its very fiber. The substructure of the body of a built artifact recedes as it materializes, akin to "Merleau-Ponty's project of foregrounding the body's value while explaining it as silent, structuring, concealed background."[13] An aesthetic of structured silence and ghosted figural ground marks contact of material and water, charges and suffuses the field, and intimates horizons within and beyond. As Eagleton describes it:

> As the aesthetic must travel beyond itself so must the aesthetic transcend itself, emptying itself of its authoritarian urges and offensively affirmative instincts until it leaves behind nothing but a ghostly negative imprint of itself, which is probably the nearest we shall get to truth.[14]

Light in bearing and of generous capacity, watermark as metaphorical carrier with emulative and interactive significance moves gingerly across architectures and landscapes, between biology and the city. It holds one promise of a memorably light and enduring ecological urbanism. Design impetus suggests at once a diaphanous artifact crafted with care and held by the hand up to the light and spatial agency capable of altering the flow of a watershed.

Notes

1   United States Environmental Protection Agency 1994.
2   For a definition of LID, see: http://water.epa.gov/polwaste/green/index.cfm.
3   Personal correspondence with Katherine Rinne, June 26, 2009; see also Rinne 2011.
4   For information on the NOAA Fisheries Ecotoxicology Program see: www. nwfsc.noaa.gov/research/divisions/efs/ecotox/index.cfm.
5   The term "salmon in the city" is borrowed from a series of public outreach events focusing on recent innovations in ecologically sustainable design as well as the latest research on urban stormwater run-off and

the fate of salmon. These events have been sponsored by Salmon Safe, (Portland) Metro, Portland Bureau of Environmental Services (BES), Herrera Environmental Consultants, and the University of Oregon. See www. salmonsafe.org/blog/save-date-salmon-city-2010-oct-27-portland.

6   Higgs 2003, 74.

7   For a consideration of advantages of overlapping, redundant surfaces relative to urban stormwater, see: Biomimicry Oregon 2013.

8   See Frampton 1995.

9   Beechie and Bolton 1999, 7.

10   The notion of "adaptive architectures" as described in this section builds from an ongoing research collaboration with Josh Cerra.

11   From a lecture Walter Hood delivered at the HOPES EcoDesign Conference at the University of Oregon on April 14, 2012.

12   See Merleau-Ponty 2003.

13   Shusterman 2005, 162.

14   Eagleton 1990, 362.

Narrating Architectural Futures

Laws control our lives, and they are designed to preserve a model of society based on values learned from mythology. Only after re-imagining our myths can we coherently remodel our lives, and hope to keep our society in a realistic relationship to what is actual.[1]

Often the resolution of these stories, as in any good tale, is deferred.[2]

Architectural practice is an epic performance of organizational skill in configuring systems and delivering projects into the world. Emerging issues and changing societal expectations join the ensemble continually and shape new patterns of practice. Not without warning the profession finds itself confronting the unprecedented: a spiral of worsening environmental problems that defy a pattern – that seem incapable of full internalization – and misalignments between trajectories of innovation and rapidly changing biophysical conditions. In commanding the architect's full attention, empowering technologies for simulating and predicting state-of-the-art high-performance buildings leave unexamined deep ecological uncertainties. Philosopher Michel Serres warns:

But now we encounter something new. At the borders of effective and precise knowledge, and at the limits of rational intervention, we find not only ignorance or error but mortal danger. Knowing is no longer enough.[3]

In *The Three Ecologies*, Felix Guattari provides a clue to what might constitute an appropriate way for architecture to respond to these enigmatic circumstances at the borders of control: "At the heart of all ecological praxes there is an a-signifying rupture, in which the catalysts of existential change are close at hand, but lack expressive support from the assemblages of enunciation."[4]

The rupture or breach (gap) is the impetus for a temporary slowing down of Latour's cadence and the making of space for thoughts and for others to generate new and principled expressive assemblages. Designers can assume a more constructive position by attending to how environmental sensibilities inhabit descriptions of their work, how the stories they tell influence the sway of the realized and concrete, and how ecological destabilization lays bare the necessity of devising and securing new ethical and aesthetic commitments. Architecture as both practice and narrative finds affinity with Robin Kirkpatrick's memorable reflection on the enduring contribution of Dante:

> **Narrative here is not simply a vehicle for Dante's ethical principles. On the contrary, it is the very form in which these principles are to be practiced. Through time we aim to work towards the good in precisely the way that we aim to sustain a coherent story.**[5]

In order to face the challenges of environmental change while fulfilling aspirations for working for the good life, William Kittredge would urge the architect to muster the courage to set forth new stories of practice and to playfully deconstruct old and worn ones: "We ride stories like rafts, or lay them out on the table like maps. They always, eventually, fail, and have to be reinvented. The world is too complex for our forms ever to encompass for long."[6]

Environmental writer Michael P. Cohen calls for a dismantling of myths (rafts), or at least cautions against taking for granted the way they propel forward and inhabit our assumptions: "Narratives use each other, and later ones have often absorbed the language, structure, and premises of earlier stories."[7] Lastly, anthropologist Hugh Brody speaks to the value of narratives that do not achieve firm resolution, that play in the fields of ambiguity. In *The Other Side of Eden*, Brody describes the beliefs and mores of the Inuit of the Canadian Arctic and remarks: "Subtlety of expression and habitual equivocation are ways of keeping close to the truth."[8]

Corresponding to a hierarchy theory of ecosystems, an ecological narrative for architectural design equivocates by keeping in suspension multiple perspectives in relation to a project's role within dynamic systems, what stabilizes and what needs encouragement, and the productive potential of selectively intentional disruption. Through a speculative, relational aesthetics, nature, no longer a mute frame of reference, acquires the status of an active, many-faceted partner that redefines the roles of designers in their conscious efforts to shape it. Historian Simon Schama wishes to restore "to the land and climate the kind of creative unpredictability conventionally reserved for human actors."[9] Nature's reclassification prompts reassessment of the constitution of the community within which a designer operates and what inputs and feedbacks enter the process. Coming up against limits and the need to create more space in the city brings about a more outwardly oriented game of complexity and contradiction in architecture.[10] Stories bearing on an ecological contribution of an architectural undertaking assume a less heroic tenor and instead the boldly elastic ambivalence of tragicomedy.

Guattari reminds us: "There is a principle specific to ecology: it states that anything is possible – the worst disasters or the most flexible evolutions."[11] With the goal of averting catastrophe, ecologically adaptive architectures are future-oriented speculations pertaining to the carrying capacity of the city. In what ways might a work of architecture contribute to a diverse and prosperous world-to-be? How might a design intervention help assimilate forces and dampen tensions while setting in motion regimes of beneficial disturbance? Is a work of architecture a means of maintaining status quo or a more fundamental positioning of those affected? Might a work prompt, through radical resourcefulness, a redefinition of quality of life, and a more humble, less material notion of esteem?

The architect bends the current toward a willed horizon. The future as capacity to act in the present acquires shape as a result of the entailments of one's commitments. In architecture, innovations over the short term and visions of utopian futures co-determine one another. It is hard to undertake the former without an attitude toward the latter.

Projects as projections of the future are illuminated by convictions held about the meaning of events of the past (beliefs about the past are in turn swayed by the spatiality of the moment). Project narratives are thus historically mediated, hopeful, future-oriented provocations. The nature writer Barry Lopez, in speaking about dominant attitudes toward the Arctic regions of North America – although he could be referring to North America more generally – claims: "Our intimacy lacks historical depth, and is still largely innocent of what is obscure and subtle there" (not to mention what is fragile and fast approaching extinction there).[12] Lack of historical depth, an insufficient grasp of vicissitudes of the past, including the dynamics of environmental change and the influence of the built environment, limit the imaginary. This is precisely why environmental and urban histories as inclusive and spatially relevant enterprises may be enabling for designers, especially those histories examining material culture at the intersection of shared social beliefs and practices and changing ecological conditions.

As with models of ecology, priorities of the moment frame observations of past events, primary influences, and the stability of the system inherited. If the image of history is its lesson, the particular set of ecological orientations addressed here suggest a hierarchically situationist view, one that discerns tendencies of entropic loosening and increasing structural complexity occurring simultaneously. Processes form rifts that coerce propitious new assemblages into being, ones that carry seeds of productive future instability. Depth of awareness of histories of natures–cultures facilitates capacity to reconcile forces seeming to operate at different frequencies and intensities. History for the designer is less a source of authority and more a fantastically rich reserve of possibility; events in the past are stimulants for novel, self-conscious action.

The situationist outlook provides the temporal equivalent of Behnisch's interest in a shimmering through of varying densities and attentiveness to the overlooked. It corresponds additionally to Deleuze's notion of "difference and repetition", where difference repeats, and where repetition reveals difference, familiar conditions never before seen.[13] According to François Dosse: "Deleuze and Guattari were not abolishing history but rather a form of historical teleology that they were replacing with the plurality of spatial logics."[14] One can debate what, if anything, truly returns, rates of flux and transformation, and how aggressively to reshape conditions and where. Designers may seek to meet massive contextual changes with massively ambitious projects for rebuilding the environment.[15] Others may envision a more modest scenario of assisting human and ecological systems and events through built interventions as restrained framings (furnishings, refrains,[16] and watermarks); acts bold yet graceful in their ethical circumscription, suggesting not nostalgic reversion but rather the grafting of elements of the past and the latest advances in technology in fashioning new worlds.

Architectures of inventive adaptation in the service of life follow precisely from dialog with those who speak the world by opening to it: ecologists, landscape architects, artists, environmental historians, philosophers, and others. Extending outward to the unfamiliar leads to intimacy of shared ethos and generation of new metaphorical scaffolds. Collaborative narrative-building in shaping the ecological potential of architecture is instantiated through inventive, concerned description of the kind of world – fragile, powerful, efficiently abundant, and fantastically earthbound – one sees value in shaping. The urban environments designers create bear enormously on the devotions and attentions felt toward those who dwell there, the ability of nonhuman species to flourish, and the dexterity and kindling of our imaginary.

Notes

1   Kittredge 1987, 64.
2   Cohen 1998, 5.
3   Serres 1992, 86.
4   Guattari 2000, 45.
5   Kirkpatrick 2007, xxvi.
6   Kittredge 2000, 9.
7   Cohen 1998, xxi.
8   Brody 2000, 235.
9   Schama 1995, 13.
10 See Venturi 1977; this externalization leads to decorated sheds of a different nature.

11 Guattari 2000, 66.

12 Lopez 1986, 245.

13 Deleuze 1994

14 Dosse 2010, 509.

15 See Mau *et al.* 2004.

16 "Refrains" as used here builds from Deleuze and Guattari's writings (see 1987, 310–350: chapter 11 "Of the Refrain") and pertains to both "desisting from" and "a group of verses repeated at intervals."

Bibliography

Agamben, Giorgio. 1998. *Homo Sacer: Sovereign Power and Bare Life.*
Translated by Daniel Heller-Roazan. Stanford, CA: Stanford University Press
(original Italian edition 1995).

Agamben, Giorgio. 2004. *The Open: Man and Animal.* Translated by Kevin
Attell. Stanford, CA: Stanford University Press (original Italian edition
2002).

American Heritage Dictionary. Second College Edition. 1982. Boston: Houghton
Mifflin Company.

Bachelard, Gaston. 1994. *The Poetics of Space.* Translated by Maria Jolas.
Boston: Beacon Press (original French edition 1958).

Barbour, Michael G. 1996. "Ecological Fragmentation in the Fifties." In
Uncommon Ground: Rethinking the Human Place in Nature. Edited by
William Cronon. New York: W.W. Norton and Company: 233–255.

Baxandall, Michael. 1985. *Patterns of Intention: On the Historical Explanation of
Pictures.* New Haven, CT: Yale University Press.

Beechie, Tim, and Bolton, Susan. 1999. "An Approach to Restoring Salmonid
Habitat-Forming Processes in Pacific Northwest Watersheds." *Fisheries* 24(4):
6–15.

Benyus, Janine. 1997. *Biomimicry: Innovation Inspired by Nature.* New York:
Harper Collins.

Berleant, Arnold. 1992. *The Aesthetics of Environment.* Philadelphia: Temple
University Press.

Berry, Don. 2004. *Trask.* Corvallis: Oregon State University Press (original edition
1960).

Biomimicry Oregon. 2013. *Nature's Strategy for Managing Stormwater in the
Willamette Valley: Genius of Place Stormwater Project Report.* http://oregon.
biomimics.net/genius-of-place-process-report.

Booth, Wayne C. 1978. "Metaphor as Rhetoric: The Problem of Evaluation."

In *On Metaphor*, edited by Sheldon Sacks. Chicago: University of Chicago Press: 47–70.

Bourriaud, Nicholas. 2002. *Relational Aesthetics*. Translated by Simon Pleasance and Fronza Woods with the participation of Mathieu Copeland. Dijon: Les presses du réel. 1998.

Brayer, Marie-Ange. 2003. "On the Surface of the Earth, in Search of the Chorographic Body." In *Archilab's Earth Buildings*, edited by Marie-Ange Brayer and Beatrice Siminot. London: Thames and Hudson: 12–19.

Brody, Hugh. 2000. *The Other Side of Eden: Hunters, Farmers and the Shaping of the World*. Vancouver: Douglas and McIntyre.

Brown, Brenda, Harkness, Terry, and Johnston, Doug. 1998. "Eco-Revelatory Design: Nature Constructed/Nature Revealed: Guest Editors' Introduction." *Landscape Journal Special Issue*. 17: ix.

Brown, G.Z. 1990. "Desirable Interface Characteristics of Knowledge-Based Energy Software Used by Architects." In *Proceedings of the American Society for Heating, Refrigerating and Air Conditioning Engineers*. Saint Louis: 1–2.

Calloway, Colin. 2003. *One Vast Winter Count: The Native American West Before Lewis and Clark*. Lincoln: University of Nebraska Press.

Calvino, Italo. 1992. *Six Memos for the Next Millennium*. Translated by Patrick Creagh. London: Jonathan Cape (originally published 1988).

Campbell, Bruce H. 2004. *Restoring Rare Native Habitats in the Willamette Valley: A Landowner's Guide for Restoring Oak Woodlands, Wetlands, Prairies, and Bottomland Hardwood and Riparian Forests*. Washington, DC: Defenders of Wildlife.

Carlson, Allen. 2000. *Aesthetics and the Environment: The Appreciation of Nature, Art and Architecture*. London: Routledge.

Carroll, Sean B. 2005. *Endless Forms Most Beautiful: The New Science of Evo Devo and the Making of the Animal Kingdom*. New York: W.W. Norton and Company.

Casey, Edward S. 1993. *Getting Back into Place: Toward a Renewed Understanding of the Place World*. Bloomington: Indiana University Press.

Casey, Edward S. 1997. *The Fate of Place: A Philosophical History*. Berkeley: University of California Press.

Cerra, Josh, and Muller, Brook. 2007. "Catalytic Interdisciplinarity: Ecological Restoration in the Architectural Design Studio." *Proceedings of the Association of Collegiate Schools of Architecture Annual Meeting*: 353–360.

Cerra, Josh, McGinley, Shannon, and Muller, Brook. 2008. "Building an Arc: Architecture, Biodiversity and the City." *Proceedings of the Association of Collegiate Schools of Architecture Annual Meeting*: 275–281.

Cohen, Michael P. 1998. *A Garden of Bristlecones: Tales of Change in the Great Basin*. Reno: University of Nevada Press.

Cohen, Ted. 1978. "Metaphor and the Cultivation of Intimacy." In *On Metaphor*, edited by Sheldon Sacks. Chicago: University of Chicago Press: 1–10.

Coolidge, Matthew. 2000. *Route 58: A Cross-Section of California.* Culver City, CA: Center for Land Use Interpretation.

Corner, James. 1997. "Ecology and Landscape as Agents of Creativity." In *Ecological Design and Planning*, edited by George E. Thompson and Frederick R. Steiner. New York: John Wiley and Sons: 80–108.

Coyne, Richard, Snodgrass, Adrian, and Martin, David. 1994. "Metaphors in the Design Studio." *Journal of Architectural Education*. Volume 48: 113–125.

Davis, Howard. 1999. *The Culture of Building*. New York: Oxford University Press.

Dawkins, Richard. 2004. *The Ancestors' Tale: The Dawn of Evolution*. Boston: Houghton Mifflin Co.

Deleuze, Gilles. 1993. *The Fold: Leibniz and the Baroque.* Translated by Tom Conley. Minneapolis: University of Minnesota Press (original French edition 1988).

Deleuze, Gilles. 1994. Difference and Repetition. Translated by Paul Patton. New York: Columbia University Press (original French edition 1968).

Deleuze, Gilles, and Guattari, Felix. 1987. *A Thousand Plateaus: Capitalism and Schizophrenia.* Translated by Brian Massumi. Minneapolis: University of Minnesota Press (original French edition 1980).

Deleuze, Gilles, and Guattari, Felix. 1994. *What Is Philosophy?* Translated by Hugh Tomlinson and Graham Burchell. New York: Columbia University Press (original French edition 1991).

Dempster, Beth. 2007. "Boundarylessness: Introducing a Systems Heuristic for Conceptualizing Complexity." In *Nature's Edge: Boundary Explorations in Ecological Theory and Practice*, edited by Charles S. Brown and Ted Toadvine. Albany: State University of New York Press: 93–110.

Dewey, John. 1980. *Art as Experience*. New York: Perigee Books (original edition 1934).

Dewey, John. 2002. *Human Nature and Conduct*. Mineola, NY: Dover Publications (original edition 1922).

Dosse, Francois. 2010. *Gilles Deleuze and Felix Guattari: Interesting Lives*. Paris: Editions La Découverte (original French edition 2007).

Eagleton, Terry. 1990. *The Ideology of the Aesthetic*. Oxford, UK: Basil Blackwell.

Eastman, Chuck. 2009. "What is BIM?" *A+U Special Issue: Architectural Transformations via BIM*. Tokyo: a+u Publishing Co.: 16–17.

Evans, James P. 2007. "Wildlife Corridors: An Urban Political Ecology." *Local Environment* 12: 129–152.

Evans, Robin. 1997. *Translations from Drawing to Building and Other Essays*. Cambridge, MA: MIT Press.

Flannery, Tim. 2001. *Eternal Frontier: An Ecological History of North America and Its Peoples*. New York: Atlantic Monthly Press.

Focillon, Henri. 1992. *The Life of Forms in Art*. Translated by Charles B. Hogan and George Kubler. New York: Zone Books (original French edition 1935).

Foreman, Dave. 2004. *Rewilding North America: A Vision For Conservation in the 21st Century*. Washington, DC: Island Press.

Forman, Richard T.T. 2002. "The Missing Catalyst: Design and Planning with Ecology Roots." In *Ecology and Design: Frameworks for Learning*, edited by Bart R. Johnson and Kristina Hill. Washington, DC: Island Press: 85–109.

Forsyth, Tim. 2003. *Critical Political Ecology: The Politics of Environmental Science*. London: Routledge.

Fox Keller, Evelyn. 1995. *Refiguring Life: Metaphors of Twentieth Century Biology*. New York: Columbia University Press.

Fraker, Harrison. 1984 (April). "Formal Speculations on Thermal Diagrams." *Progressive Architecture*: 104.

Frampton, Kenneth. 1995. *Studies in Tectonic Culture: The Poetics of Construction in Nineteenth and Twentieth Century Architecture*. Cambridge, MA: MIT Press.

Gadamer, Hans-Georg. 2004. *Truth and Method*. Translated by Joel Weinsheimer and Donald G. Marshall. London: Continuum (original edition 1975).

Geertz, Clifford. 2000. *The Interpretation of Cultures*. New York: Basic Books.

Gonzalez, Valerie. 2001. *Beauty and Islam: Aesthetics in Islamic Art and Architecture*. London: I.B. Tauris Publishers.

Gross, Matthias. 2003. *Inventing Nature: Ecological Restoration by Public Experiments*. Lanham, MD: Lexington Books.

Gross, Matthias. 2010. *Ignorance and Surprise*. Cambridge, MA: MIT Press.

Guattari, Felix. 2000. *The Three Ecologies*. Translated by Ian Pindar and Paul Sutton. London: Continuum/The Athlone Press (original French edition 1989).

Guy, Simon, and Farmer, Graham. 2001. "Reinterpreting Sustainable Architecture: The Place of Technology." *Journal of Architectural Education* 54: 140–148.

Guy, Simon, and Moore, Steven A. 2005. "Introduction: The Paradoxes of Sustainable Architecture." In *Sustainable Architectures: Cultures and Natures in Europe and North America*, edited by Simon Guy and Steven A. Moore. New York: Spon Press: 1–12.

Habraken, NJ 1998. *The Structure of the Ordinary: Form and Control in the Built Environment*. Cambridge, MA: MIT Press.

Haila, Yrjo, and Levins, Richard. 1992. *Humanity and Nature: Ecology, Science and Society*. London: Pluto Press.

Hansen, Mark B.N. 2005. "The Embryology of the (In)visible." In *The Cambridge Companion to Merleau-Ponty*, edited by Taylor Carman and Mark B.N. Hansen. Cambridge, UK: Cambridge University Press: 231–264.

Harries, Karsten. 1998. *The Ethical Function of Architecture*. Cambridge, MA: MIT Press.

Hellmund, Paul Caewood, and Smith, Daniel Somers. 2006. *Designing Greenways: Sustainable Landscapes for Nature and People*. Washington, DC: Island Press.

Hester, Randolph. 2006. *Design for Ecological Democracy.* Cambridge, MA: MIT Press.

Higgs, Eric. 2003. *Nature by Design: People, Natural Process and Ecological Restoration.* Cambridge, MA: MIT Press.

Holl, Steven, Pallasmaa, Juhani, and Perez-Gomez, Alberto. 1994. "Questions of Perception: Phenomenology of Architecture." *Architecture and Urbanism Special Issue.* Tokyo: a+u Publishing Co.

Holling, C.S. 1973. "Resilience and the Stability of Ecological Systems." *Annual Review of Ecology and Systematics* 4: 1–23.

Hubbell, Stephen P. 2001. *The Unified Neutral Theory of Biodiversity and Biogeography* (Monographs in Population Biology #32). Princeton, NJ: Princeton University Press.

Jackson. Jeremy B.C., Kirby, Michael X., Berger, Wolfgang H., Bjorndal, Karen A., Botsford, Louis W., Bourque, Bruce J., *et al.* 2001. "Historical Overfishing and the Recent Collapse of Coastal Ecosystems." *Science* 293 (5530): 629–637.

James, Vincent, and Yoos, Jennifer. 2006. *VJAA.* Princeton, NJ: Princeton Architectural Press.

Johnson, Bart R., and Hill, Kristina. 2002. "Introduction: Toward Landscape Realism." In *Ecology and Design: Frameworks for Learning,* edited by Bart R. Johnson and Kristina Hill. Washington, DC: Island Press: 1–26.

Johnson, Mark. 1987. *The Body in the Mind: The Bodily Basis of Meaning, Imagination, and Reason.* Chicago: University of Chicago Press.

Kellert, Stephen R. 2005. *Building for Life: Designing and Understanding the Human–Nature Connection.* Washington, DC: Island Press.

Kingsland, Sharon E. 1991 "Foundational Papers: Defining Ecology as a Science." In *Foundations in Ecology: Classic Papers with Commentaries,* edited by Leslie A. Neal and James H. Brown. Chicago: University of Chicago Press: 1–13.

Kirkpatrick, Robin. 2003. "Introduction to Dante's *Paradiso.*" In Dante's *Paradiso* translated by Robin Kirkpatrick. London: Penguin Classics: xiii–lxiv.

Kirkpatrick, Robin. 2007. "Introduction to Dante's *Purgatorio.*" In Dante's *Purgatorio* translated by Robin Kirkpatrick. London: Penguin Classics: xi–lix.

Kittredge, William. 1987. *Owning It All.* Saint Paul, MN: Graywolf Press.

Kittredge, William. 2000. *The Nature of Generosity*. New York: Alfred A. Knopf.

Knudson, Kaarin, and Muller, Brook. 2009. "Landscape Metaphors, Ecological Imperatives and Architectural Design." *Proceedings of the Association of Collegiate Schools of Architecture Annual Meeting*: 225–231.

Koolhaas, Rem. 1996. "Beyond Delirious." In *Theorizing a New Agenda for Architecture: An Anthology of Architectural Theory 1965–1995*, edited by Kate Nesbitt. New York: Princeton Architectural Press: 332–336.

Kristeller, Paul Oskar. 1943. *The Philosophy of Marsilio Ficino*. New York: Columbia University Press.

Lakoff, George. 2006. *Whose Freedom? The Battle over America's Most Important Idea*. New York: Picador.

Lakoff, George, and Johnson, Mark. 1980. *Metaphors We Live By*. Chicago: University of Chicago Press.

Latour, Bruno. 1993. *We Have Never Been Modern*. Translated by Catherine Porter. Cambridge, MA: Harvard University Press (original edition in French 1991).

Latour, Bruno. 2004. *The Politics of Nature: How to Bring the Sciences into Democracy*. Translated by Catherine Porter. Cambridge, MA: Harvard University Press (original edition in French 2004).

Latour, Bruno, and Yaneva, Albena. 2008. "80 Networks Essay 1: Give Me a Gun and I Will Make All Buildings Move: An Ant's View of Architecture." In *Architecture*, edited by R. Geister. Basel: Birkhauser: 80–89.

Leatherbarrow, David. 2000. *Uncommon Ground: Architecture, Technology, Topography*. Cambridge: MIT Press.

Lévi-Strauss, Claude. 1963. *Totemism*. Translated by Rodney Needham. Boston: Beacon Press (original French edition 1962).

Lévi-Strauss, Claude. 1966. *The Savage Mind*. Chicago: University of Chicago Press (original French edition 1962).

Lewontin, Richard. 2000. *The Triple Helix: Gene, Organism and Environment*. Cambridge, MA: Harvard University Press. 2000.

Littlefield, David. 2012. "Bankside Urban Forest." *Architectural Design Special Issue: London (Re)Generation* 82(1): 44–49.

Lopez, Barry. 1986. *Arctic Dreams: Imagination and Desire in a Northern Landscape*. Toronto: Bantam Books.

Lundholm, Jeremy T. 2006. "Green Roofs and Facades: A Habitat Template Approach." *Urban Habitats* 4: 1–15.

Mallinson, Helen. 2004. "Metaphors of Experience: The Voice of Air." *Philosophical Forum* 35(2): 161–177.

Mau, Bruce, Leonard, Jennifer, and Institute Without Borders. 2004. *Massive Change*. New York: Phaidon Press.

McGinley, Shannon. 2008. "Biodiversity and the City: Habitat Integrated Architecture in the Urban Landscape." University of Oregon Master of Landscape Architecture thesis.

Merleau-Ponty, Maurice. 2003. *Nature: Course Notes from the Collège de France*. Translated by Robert Vallier. Evanston, IL: Northwestern University Press (original French edition 1968).

Meyer, Stephen. 2006. *The End of the Wild*. Cambridge, MA: MIT Press.

Montgomery, David. 2003. *King of Fish: The Thousand-Year Run of Salmon*. Boulder, CO: Westview Press.

Moore, Steven A., and Wilson, Barbara B. 2009. "Contested Construction of Green Building Codes in North America: The Case of the Alley Flat Initiative." *Urban Studies* 46(12): 2617–2641.

Mugerauer, Robert 2004. "Deleuze and Guattari's Return to Science as a Basis for Environmental Philosophy." In *Rethinking Nature: Essays in Environmental Philosophy*, edited by Bruce V. Foltz and Robert Frodeman. Bloomington: Indiana University Press: 180–204.

Nabhan, Gary Paul. 1997. *Cultures of Habitat: On Nature, Culture, and Story*. Washington, DC: Counterpoint.

Nassauer, Joan Iverson. 1995. "Messy Ecosystems, Orderly Frames." *Landscape Journal* 14(2): 161–170.

Nassauer, Joan Iverson. 1997. "Cultural Sustainability: Aligning Aesthetics and Ecology." In *Placing Nature: Culture and Landscape Ecology*, edited by Joan Iverson Nassauer. Washington, DC: Island Press: 65–84.

Norton, Bryan. 1987. *Why Preserve Natural Variety?* Princeton, NJ: Princeton University Press.

Norton, Bryan. 2005. *Sustainability: A Philosophy of Adaptive Ecosystem Management*. Chicago: University of Chicago Press.

O'Neill, R.V., DeAngelis, D.L., Waide, J.B., and Allen, T.F.H. 1986. *A Hierarchical*

Concept of Ecosystems (Monographs in Population Biology 23). Princeton, NJ: Princeton University Press.

Perez-Gomez, Alberto. 2006. *Built upon Love: Architectural Longing after Ethics and Aesthetics*. Cambridge, MA: MIT Press.

Piano, Renzo. 1997. *Logbook*. Milan: Moncelli Press.

Pickett, S.T.A., and White, P.S. 1985. *The Ecology of Natural Disturbance and Patch Dynamics*. Orlando, FL: Academic Press.

Pickett, S.T.A., Cadenasso, Mary L., Grove, J. Morgan, Groffman, Peter M., Band, Lawrence, Boone, Christopher G., *et al.* 2008. "Beyond Urban Legends: An Emerging Framework of Urban Ecology, as Illustrated by the Baltimore Ecosystem Study." *BioScience* 58(2): 139–150.

Princeton Architectural Press. 2002. *City Limits: Young Architects 3*. New York: Princeton Architectural Press and the Architectural League of New York.

Proctor, James D., and Larson, Brendon M.H. 2005. "Ecology, Complexity, and Metaphor." *Bioscience* 55(12): 1065–1068.

Pulliam, Harold, and Johnson, Bart R. 2002. "Ecology's New Paradigm: What Does It Offer Designers and Planners?" In *Ecology and Design: Frameworks for Learning*, edited by Bart R. Johnson and Kristina Hill. Washington, DC: Island Press: 51–84.

Rees, William, and Wackernagel, Mathis. 2008. "Urban Ecological Footprints: Why Cities Cannot be Sustainable – and Why They Are a Key to Sustainability." In *Urban Ecology: An International Perspective on the Interactions between Humans and Nature*, edited by J.M. Marzluff, Eric Shulenberger, Wilfried Endlicher, Marina Alberti, Gordon Bradley, Clare Ryan, *et al.* New York: Springer (originally published in *Environmental Impact Assessment Review* 16: 223–248).

Ricoeur, Paul. 1977. *The Rule of Metaphor: Multi-Disciplinary Studies of the Creation of Meaning in Language*. Translated by Robert Czerny. Toronto: University of Toronto Press (original French edition 1975).

Ricoeur, Paul. 1978. "The Metaphorical Process as Cognition, Imagination, and Feeling." In *On Metaphor*, edited by Sheldon Sacks. Chicago: University of Chicago Press: 141–157.

Rinne, Katherine. 2011. *The Waters of Rome: Aqueducts, Fountains and the Birth of the Baroque City*. New Haven, CT: Yale University Press.

Rorty, Richard. 1991. *Essays on Heidegger and Other Philosophical Papers*, Volume 2. Cambridge, UK: Cambridge University Press.

Rorty, Richard. 1999. "A World Without Substances or Essences." In *Philosophy of Social Hope*. New York: Penguin Books: 47–71.

Rosenzweig, Michael L. 2003. *Win–Win Ecology: How the Earth's Species Can Survive in the Midst of Human Enterprise*. Oxford, UK: Oxford University Press.

Scalbert, Irenee. 2004. *A Right to Difference: The Architecture of Jean Renaudie*. London: AA Publications.

Schama, Simon. 1995. *Landscape and Memory*. New York: Alfred A. Knopf.

Schoen, Donald. 1987. *Educating the Reflective Practitioner*. San Francisco: Jossey-Bass Publishers.

Serres, Michel. 1992 *The Natural Contract*. Translated by Elizabeth MaCarthur and William Paulson. Ann Arbor: University of Michigan Press (original French edition 1990).

Shepard, Paul. 1998. *Coming Home to the Pleistocene*. Washington, DC: Island Press.

Shusterman. Richard. 2005. "The Silent, Limping Body of Philosophy." In *The Cambridge Companion to Merleau-Ponty*, edited by Taylor Carman and Mark B.N. Hansen. Cambridge: Cambridge University Press: 151–180.

Smout Allen. 2007. *Augmented Landscapes*. Pamphlet Architecture 28. New York: Princeton Architectural Press.

Snyder, Gary. 1990. *The Practice of the Wild*. Washington, DC: Shoemaker and Hoard.

Solomon, Daniel. 2003. *Global City Blues*. Washington, DC: Island Press.

Spence, Rory. 1998. "Heightened Senses." *Architectural Review* 203(1214): 69–76.

Steiner, George. 1998. *After Babel: Aspects of Language and Translation*, 3rd edition. Oxford, UK: Oxford University Press.

Stilgoe, John. 2003. "Land Fear: Wildness and the Bewilderment of the City Dweller." *Architecture Boston*. March/April: 20–21.

Takacs, David. 1996. *The Idea of Biodiversity: Philosophies of Paradise*. Baltimore, MD: Johns Hopkins University Press.

Taleb, Nicholas Nassim. 2007. *The Black Swan: The Impact of the Highly Improbable*. New York: Random House.

Tanizaki, Jun'ichiro. 1977. *In Praise of Shadows*. Translated by Thomas Harper and Edward Seidensticker. Stony Creek, CT: Leete's Island Books (original Japanese edition 1933).

Treib, Marc. 1979. "Traces upon the Land: The Formalistic Landscape." *Architectural Association Quarterly* 2(4): 28–39.

United States Environmental Protection Agency. 1994. *What Is Nonpoint Source (NPS) Pollution. Questions and Answers*. EPA-841-F094-005. www.epa.gov/owow/nps.qa.html.

Varela, Francisco J., Thompson, Evan, and Rosch, Eleanor. 1991. *The Embodied Mind: Cognitive Science and Human Experience*. Cambridge, MA: MIT Press.

Venturi, Robert. 1977. *Complexity and Contradiction in Architecture*. New York: Museum of Modern Art.

Von Uexküll, Jakob. 1957. "A Stroll Through the Worlds of Animals and Men: A Picture Book of Invisible Worlds." In *Instinctive Behavior: The Development of a Modern Concept* edited and translated by Claire H. Schiller. New York: International Universities Press: 5–80.

Whiteside, Kerry. 2002. *Divided Natures: French Contributions to Political Ecology*. Cambridge, MA: MIT Press.

Wilde, Oscar. 1969. "The Decay of Lying: An Observation." In *The Artist as Critic: Critical Writings of Oscar Wilde*. Edited by Richard Ellman. New York: Random House: 290–320 (original published in *Intentions* 1891).

Williams, Raymond. 1973. *The Country and the City*. New York: Oxford University Press.

Wood, David. 2005. *The Step Back: Ethics and Politics After Deconstruction*. Albany: State University of New York Press.

Wood, David. 2006. "On the Way to Econstruction." *Environmental Philosophy* 3(1): 35–46.

Yeang, Ken. 2006. *Ecodesign: A Manual for Ecological Design*. London: Wiley Academy.

Young, Iris Marion. 1990. *Justice and the Politics of Difference*. Princeton, NJ: Princeton University Press.

Yui, Leonard. 2010. "Ecological Aesthetics in Architecture: A Deadwood Metaphor." University of Oregon Master of Architecture thesis.

Zacks, Stephen. 2007. "The Magic Lantern." *Metropolis* 26(7): 97–103, 147–148.

Credits

Portions of Chapters 4 and 7 are excerpted from an essay coauthored with Kaarin Knudson, "Landscape Metaphors, Ecological Imperatives and Architectural Design," *Proceedings of the 2009 Association of Collegiate Schools of Architecture Annual Meeting.*

Portions of Chapter 8 are excerpted from an essay coauthored with Josh Cerra and Shannon McGinley, "Building an Arc: Architecture, Biodiversity and the City," *Proceedings of the 2008 Association of Collegiate Schools of Architecture Annual Meeting.*

Portions of Chapter 2 are excerpted from an essay coauthored with Josh Cerra, "Catalytic Interdisciplinarity: Ecological Restoration in the Architectural Design Studio," *Proceedings of the 2007 Association of Collegiate Schools of Architecture Annual Meeting.*

With kind permission from Springer Science+Business Media BV, portions of Chapters 4 and 6 are excerpted from "Environmental Receptivity and Architectural Design," in *Symbolic Landscapes*, edited by Gary Backhaus and John Murungi. New York: Springer Science+Business Media, 2009.

Portions of Chapter 10 are excerpted from "Continuity of Singularities: Architecture, Ecology and the Aesthetics of Restorative Orders," in *Environmental Philosophy: Special Double Issue: Environmental Aesthetics and Ecological Restoration* 4(1/2) (2007).

Portions of Chapter 4 and the epilogue are excerpted from "Myths of Knowledge Creation in Sustainable Architecture," *Proceedings of the 2012 International Association for the Study of Traditional Environments Conference "The Myth of Tradition."*

Portions of Chapters 5 and 11 are excerpted from "EcoArchitectural Machines," *Proceedings of the 2012 Association of Collegiate Schools of Architecture Annual Meeting.*

Portions of Chapters 1 and 3 are excerpted from "Architectures of Beneficial Disturbance: Ecological Models and Architectural Explorations in a Post-Linguistic World," *Proceedings of the 2011 Association of Collegiate Schools of Architecture Annual Meeting.*

All illustrations are by the author.

Index

Page numbers in **bold** denote figures.